Supergirls
Speak Out

....

*Inside the Secret Crisis
of Overachieving Girls*

....

Liz Funk

A Touchstone Book
Published by Simon & Schuster
New York   London   Toronto   Sydney

For my sister, Allie,

who is as perfect as a girl can get
without it being a cause for concern
and who has always unselfishly cared
about the well-being of others.

Touchstone
A Division of Simon & Schuster, Inc.
1230 Avenue of the Americas
New York, NY 10020

First Touchstone trade paperback edition March 2009

TOUCHSTONE and colophon are registered trademarks
of Simon & Schuster, Inc.

For information about special discounts for bulk purchases, please contact
Simon & Schuster Special Sales at 1-800-456-6798
or business@simonandschuster.com.

Designed by Joy O'Meara

Manufactured in the United States of America

1   3   5   7   9   10   8   6   4   2

Library of Congress Cataloging-in-Publication Data
Funk, Liz.
Supergirls speak out : inside the secret crisis
of overachieving girls / Liz Funk.
p. cm.
1. Young women—Psychology. 2. Success. 3. Sex role. I. Title
HQ1233.F86 2009
155.6'5—dc22   208017408

ISBN-13: 978-1-4165-6263-4
ISBN-10:   1-4165-6263-X

Acknowledgments

There are so many people who have contributed to this book and who have nurtured me as both a writer and a person. Twelve-point font probably can't do justice to the deep feelings of gratitude that I feel, but I'll give it a shot!

I probably owe the first thanks to Courtney Martin, who really mentored me in the publishing industry and in feminist pursuits, and who introduced me to my agent. Naturally, I want to thank my agent, Wendy Sherman, who brought such energy and dedication to our work together and gives all her work such flair. I want to thank my editor, Michelle Howry, who has been a blast to work with and has made every step of this book fun and exciting, in addition to giving me constant guidance, insightful comments, and mentoring. A big thanks to Meghan Stevenson, another great editor at Touchstone Fireside, who helped so much throughout the course of this book. Also, thank you to Ellen Silberman for her incredible work on the publicity and promotion of this book.

The "stars" of this book: Katie, Pegah, Allie, Leah, and Yolanda were endlessly open to the strangeness of letting a 19-year-old journalist follow them around. You were all so much fun to hang out with . . . and I promise you, you all have incredibly fascinating lives. Thank you to Sherri Taylor, a fantastic educator at Syracuse University, for being so willing to allow me to participate in the School Press Institute and also for organizing the summer camp that made me certain that writing was my calling. Big thank-yous are also owed to Cliff Odell and Dr. Bonnie Morris for making my connections with some of our other main characters possible. Also, thank you to each and every young woman and expert who agreed to be interviewed: it was really invigorating to hear all of their stories and insight, and I so appreciate their candidness. Thank you to "Jenna," who didn't officially lend her story to this book, but whose story and life have influenced more than just a couple of girls. Also, a huge thanks to Christina Foglia for helping me find such great sources.

During the course of researching, writing, and promoting this book, I've met so many amazing writers and experts who have been a blast to get to know and work with, especially Amber Madison, Hannah Seligson, and Leora Tanenbaum. And a big thank-you to Cathy Wasserman for helping me—and Supergirls everywhere!—become "open to exploring the mystery of their lives." I've had other really inspiring mentors, especially Melissa Walker, Laura Sessions Stepp, Jamia Wilson, Erin Matson, and Marissa Meltzer: thank you all for the amazing work you've done not just for me, but for women and culture, too.

I've had some truly inspiring professors and teachers along the way, especially Jan Geyer, Jai Misir, Jonathan Silverman, and Sid Ray, who have all given me fantastic advice about writing and life. Also, a big thanks to Mrs. Bills, Mr. Streifer, Ms. Griffin, Ms. Levy, Ms. Riddell, and Mr. Diefendorf, the people who so inspired me in high school who I've never formally thanked but should have.

A big thanks to the members of my writers' groups and book clubs: you all have helped shape me and figured out how to pare down my writing and get stuff published . . . plus, you make work so much fun!

I can't explain how lucky I am to have been so openly welcomed to the "progressive family" at Young People For, and I can't thank everyone at People for the American Way Foundation enough, especially Rachel Burrows and Iara Peng! Big thanks also belong to Erin McNamara, Sonal Bains, and Caroline Ross, not only for the change they provoke, but more importantly, for being such great friends!

My friends are really my lifeline, and there are no words to describe how much I appreciate their willingness to accept my quirks and love me anyway. Thanks so much to Michele, Cheri, Lauren, Kate, Rikki, Blair, and Bridget: you gals consistently amaze me with your grace and beauty. Thanks to Natascha for helping me loosen up, stop taking things so seriously, and have fun! A big thanks to the *Pace Press*-ers, especially Jackie Berg, Adam Reichardt, Tyler Davis, and Neelofer Qudir. Thanks to Austin and Adrian for being my most vocal fans and for always giving me such fantastic advice; thanks to Kaitlin for always knowing how to bring fun and Dave Matthews into the mix. My best friends, Tara and Hilary, have been there for me through thick and thin and always let me hijack their iPods in the car and sit in the middle whenever we go places. I couldn't wish for better best friends.

Endless thanks also belong to my family, who have been such a strong support system for me throughout my life and my writing career. Thanks so much to Grandma and Grandpa, Aunt Pat, Uncle Anthony and Aunt Kathleen, Aunt Diane, and Uncle Pete and Aunt Julie, plus the entire litter of cousins that constitutes my extended family, for being so quirky and fun, but more importantly, so loving. Although not officially family, thank you to the Smith family for being an extra support system.

Thank you to Dad for instilling creativity and a dedication to the arts in me. Thank you to Gary for teaching me to always help others in a bind. Thank you to my mom for everything she has done for me. Mom, you amaze me with your wit, your love, and your dedication to always do the right thing; I can't thank you enough for everything throughout the years and for the messages that you helped me find within *The Wizard of Oz*. Final thanks belong to my sister, Allie: Allie, you are a gem. I have always admired your dedication to others, your talent, your humor, and your zest for life. You are a role model to me and I believe to girls everywhere, and for that I dedicate my first book to you.

Contents

chapter one

The Supergirl Manifesto

Since When Is Being "Super" a Bad Thing?

....

What makes the perfect girl?
—A *Seventeen.com* article that shows guys weighing in on the
personal and physical traits that create the "perfect" female

Jenna[1] was supposedly perfect. She was the valedictorian of
her senior class—the girl whom the guys wanted to get with and
the girls wanted to be. There were rumors going around that she
had an almost perfect GPA from all four years of high school, that
the hottest guy in the senior class had a blatant crush on her, and
that she spent her vacations in Cancun tanning in a thong bikini.
She was always playing sports—she skied and ran avidly—and
she led lots of school activities. Pretty much everyone in her town
knew about her: even parents who never actually met her knew of
her personal prowess.

---

1 Some of the names and identifying characteristics of the people described in this
book have been changed.

But it's not like she was one of those mean perfect girls: she was shockingly nice and kind to everyone, even to the losers and the unpopular kids who talked to her, hoping to get that buzz from just conversing with her. She smiled constantly and dressed as though Abercrombie and Fitch's senior designer lived in her closet. She had been accepted at one of the best colleges in the country, yet rumor had it that she didn't have a major planned, because she wanted to stay open to being a doctor or an engineer or something within the humanities: she was smart and seemed interested in every subject! Plus, just to reiterate, she was one of the most beautiful young women most people had ever seen, with glossy hair and a perfect body and a kind of relaxed glow to her that made everything she did look effortless. Unfortunately, to the contrary, a week or so before graduation, she was admitted to the local psychiatric hospital for some combination of bulimia, depression, and exhaustion. And no one really knew what to say except, "I thought she was perfect."

Supergirls: they're the girls with the perfectly blow-dried, shiny hair who sit up perfectly straight while taking notes during their fourth AP class of the day, or who walk across the campus quad in perfect outfits, hand-in-hand with their fraternity president boyfriends and iPhones glued to their ears. Or they're the young women who take on extra projects at work, yet still manage to win over all of their coworkers at the watercooler and grab their boss a latte on the way in to work. And while doing all of this, there is an unsaid pressure to make it look like they're airy and energetic, like they "just wanna have fun!" Supergirls seem to have everything: the education, the boyfriends, the friends, the looks, and the awards . . . but they're probably missing some- thing, too. After all, is it really healthy for young women to aspire to appear effortlessly perfect?

As predicted, all really isn't perfect in the land of perfect girls. As poor Jenna demonstrated, the young women who appear to have it all are often about to lose it all at any given moment—or at the moment that their minds and bodies say, "Sorry, I just can't do it anymore!" While our society puts a high premium on young women doing it all and making such overachieving look easy—or, ideally, effortless—our bodies and brains can only take so much.

Growing up as a girl is a kind of weird tango today. It's about being smart, well rounded, and successful—someone your parents can brag about at family reunions and someone your friends can give glowing introductions for at dinner parties—but also still being all the things that we've understood girls to be for the past hundred or so years—amenable, self-effacing, sweet, and, of course, pretty. Trying to be powerful gets a little confusing when you have to apologize for it and make up for it . . . and making up for it is doing all the things that are considered feminine.

What makes things ever more complicated is that there's no official role for girls today: we see women as sex objects on MTV, and we see young women as professionally powerful but picking catfights and obsessing over guys on TV (ah, *Grey's Anatomy*), but most girls I spoke with said that girls were most often class president, and women now outnumber men at most of the best universities in the country. Despite women's progress, girls are raised to be "good," but because no one has any clue what "good" is today—an old-fashioned term to describe the female ideal—young women feel the push to be good at everything. So, what's a forward-thinking gal to do? Because of the media saturation in our generation, there has been a high premium put on making adolescence look fluffy and pink; college being exclusively about drinking, hookups, and getting addicted to your hair straightener; and the twenties being about wine in a box and buying throw pillows for your first apartment. It's not considered appropriate to be exploring your issues or even having crises. It's about trying to have all this confusion under control.

This perplexity gets wrapped up in the Supergirl dilemma. Shakespeare said, "All the world's a stage," and young women are really taking that to heart, trying to act as though doing everything is something they enjoy and something that comes naturally to them. They try to be occupied every minute of the day. But they're generally always in the process of fending off some serious struggles . . . and it's a secret. Girls like Jenna—and many more who you'll meet in this book—pulled it off for a few years, doing everything, pleasing everyone, and making it all look easy. Suddenly, their bodies and brains gave out on them, and they had anxiety attacks, mental breakdowns, and some severe physical problems. Whenever I chatted with a girl for my research in this book, I tried to ask her if her constant overworking ever resulted in a breakdown or a health issue . . . and almost half said yes, whether it was developing anxiety from feeling like they had so much to juggle or being urged by their therapist to pare down their activities after having a mental breakdown at school.

But if girls aren't popping Adderall or dieting for the sake of dieting, it seems like, for them, waking up in the morning just welcomes another day of agita: as one girl put it, "I hate relaxing. It's not something I do well." But what's the point of living if life is such a chore? Well, Supergirls may have answered that question in September 2007 when the U.S. Centers for Disease Control released the results of a study that found rates of suicide among

> "For girls, it's 'If I'm a cheerleader and I play violin and I'm in eight clubs and I'm a straight-A student and I have the hottest date to the prom, maybe people will like me.'"
> —Rachel, age 16

girls had risen exponentially, with a 32 percent increase among 15- to 19-year-old girls and a 76 percent increase among 10- to 14-year-old girls.

One of my good friends is a perfect girl. She's pretty, she graduated from an Ivy League college, she's skinny and well dressed, and everyone likes her. The only weird thing about her is that she doesn't drink coffee or eat spicy food. Why? She has ulcers from being so stressed! But you'd never know it looking at her. When we meet a "perfect" girl, we often wonder, "What's her secret?" But we should really be looking for different kinds of secrets: not what hair products she uses to get such shiny tresses or how she balances all her activities without ever seeming spent, but what she's trying to make up for or what she's trying to hide.

Meet the Supergirls

At 8am, in the heat of summer at Syracuse University, 16-year-old Katie, a Rome, New York, native, takes notes feverishly in a journalism course aimed toward high school students. She is working on a story for the class about an upcoming speech that the chief justice of the Supreme Court is giving at Syracuse University in the fall, and she feigns being awake in class even though she was up late for the past few nights chilling out with the other kids in the dorm. In between the seven hours of daily classes, she balances chasing down sources for her article, keeping tabs on her overcaffeinated friends, and calling her boyfriend back home.

A few months later, Allie, 19, is dodging puddles on I Street in Washington, D.C., guarded by a bubble-like clear umbrella. It's past dinnertime—she's been going all day at classes and internships—and she is still energetic and friendly. Not to mention, she has hours' worth of studying to do . . . and her focus is not even tempted by the sound of laughter from the pubs we pass where students are drinking beer. With a goal of becoming a top Washington lobbyist, nothing seems to distract her from her work.

A few weeks later, at 11am on an unseasonably cold Monday in October, Yolanda, 27, takes a break from her fancy banking job in midtown Manhattan to grab an early lunch at a nearby restaurant, where she picks at a sweet potato and chicken breast. She's attractive and curvaceous, and is checked out by several guys who are probably her peers in the industry; she doesn't notice them and is probably too busy to care. The streets outside buzz with life and activity—I'm pretty sure I saw a pack of models leaving their hotel down the street—but Yolanda is relatively focused on talking about one of her best accounts. Yolanda's job is kind of swanky: she exclusively handles private banking for individuals worth over $35 million.

In early November, Pegah, 15, eats a slice of pizza without getting grease anywhere on her outfit in a quaint pizza parlor down the street from her school in Valley Stream, New York. Her friends, virtually all in some combination of North Face fleeces, tight jeans, cheerleading skirts, and UGGs, talk about the events of the day and tomorrow's football game against the school's biggest rival. Pegah listens and tells an occasional joke, but also skims through her notes at the crowded table; this is pretty much the only time she'll "relax" the entire day, given that hours of studying are to come . . . on a Friday night!

Meanwhile, 18-year-old Leah, who chose SUNY–Albany over her pick of prestigious colleges for financial reasons, has kept busy for her entire first semester at college, filling time between classes with the Student Senate, Spanish club, and her work-study job making smoothies in the student center. She's kept so busy that she's barely seen her suitemates in her dorm, who all have plans for making the most of the other things that UAlbany has to offer, like hooking up, pledging, and joining the feminine backdrop of the noted Albany club scene. Jell-O shots, anyone? Not for Leah . . . she's prefers espresso or coffee. Although, with all the house parties and open-bar school fund-raisers she goes to, who can resist every now and then?

Dane Cook, the stand-up comedian beloved by nearly everyone in Generation Y, has this really hilarious monologue about crying. He says, "There's those times when you need to cry, a real cry. Then, as you're crying, what happens is it starts to feel good that you're crying like that, and what you do is you latch on to one phrase that you just repeat over and over again. Just something that means something to you like, 'I did my best. . . . I did my best. . . . I did my best, I did my f-cking best, I did my, my best, I did my best, I did my best, I did my best, I did my . . . best!'"

What makes Dane Cook so hilarious is that the things he says are often true, things that are in his fans' very lives. In this case, unfortunately, he hit a little too close to home. As I was spending the summer and fall following these amazing girls in high school building up their activities résumés for college and these stellar college students who just got out of the college admissions rat race (plus Yolanda, our 20-something Supergirl who luckily already graduated from McGill before kids from the United States figured out how chi-chi the school is and began flocking there, making the school even harder to get into), the same things were going on much more locally.

My younger sister and I have always had somewhat of an informal rivalry—I've always perceived her as smarter, prettier, and nicer, and I think she is occasionally annoyed by people asking her if she's "the 'writer Funk daughter' or the other one"—but we've always been extremely close, and despite our occasional jealousies, we have really rooted for each other throughout the years. Allie was in her senior year of high school when I was following our five Supergirls throughout the fall, and Allie was going where her big sis had never gone: she was shooting for the Ivy League for college. Namely, she had her sights set on Cornell. After sending in her early decision application way ahead of the deadline, Allie waited, eagerly anticipating the day in early December when she'd know. That day came, but when she checked online at exactly 5pm when the results would be posted, she found herself in a situation not unlike Dane Cook, crying and saying over and over again, "I did everything! . . . I did everything! . . . I did everything!" Needless to say, Cornell didn't hold my sister in the high esteem that I and most people in my town do (although it wasn't a full-out insult; in December they deferred her application to the spring, at which point they offered her admission . . . for sophomore year, which I perceive as both a compliment and a total bitch move at the same time).

Supergirls span time, geography, and age, but they all have one thing in common. They're all in a race to be perfect—a race in which sweatbands are stilettos, Adidas is Abercrombie, and shin splints are smiles. Unfortunately, there's no finish line, because every time they come close to the agreed endpoint, they push themselves to go faster and longer.

But I have to confess . . . I'm not just an outside observer of this Supergirl phenomenon. Although I'm working on modifying my behavior, I'm one of them.

All of Us Supergirls

I think somehow I've always been a Supergirl. In the seventh grade, I set my sights on Harvard and wanted to achieve academically. So I studied and got on the high honor roll. In the eighth grade, I got hooked on the Disney Channel show *Even Stevens;* I saw the main character, Ren Stevens, achieving in school and doing tons of extracurricular activities, and she looked really empowered! So I became an editor of the school newspaper, joined the foreign cultures club (I was president the following two years), was elected class treasurer, and wrote frequent letters to the editor of our local newspaper on social justice issues.

In the ninth grade, I became obsessed with my size and my looks, and I ended up becoming anorexic. I ate very little, ran four to six miles a day (more on some days!), and joined the school cross-country team. Although I gained the weight back, it only fueled my overachieving drive. In the tenth grade, I decided I wanted to become a writer, and I wrote screenplays, journalistic pieces, and even a full-length book; I became represented by a literary agent, and although my book was never published, I became engrossed in the inner workings of the publishing industry. In the eleventh grade, I got caught up in the college admissions fever. I worked my tail off in school and studied like a maniac for the SAT; it was actually somewhat of a heartbreaking experience, as I set a totally unrealistic goal score, and when I scored only fifty points shy of it, I couldn't even feel good about it. This was the same year that I became a progressive activist and organized protests, worked with local community service groups, and founded a feminist club for girls in my area. In the twelfth grade, I opted to attend community college for my senior year of high school in a special acceleration program, simultaneously finishing high school and starting my college coursework; this was the same year that I started freelance writing professionally.

The next year, I began my sophomore year of college in New York City (so much for Harvard) and began writing for more prestigious newspapers and magazines, learned how to network, and got a book deal; not to mention, New York City presented its own new opportunities and challenges, like parties, the unofficial lack of a legal drinking age, and shopping and sightseeing that was ultimately quite time-consuming.

Now, I'm 19 and still on the go. I have a writing career I'm fairly satisfied with, I have great friends, I have a supportive and loving family, I'm going to graduate from college next year at the age of 20, and I have finally achieved the perfect shade of blonde for my hair (and to emphasize how sexist this situation is, that's probably the achievement I'm most proud of). But I don't mean to come off as cocky or ostentatious, because what underlies all of these "accomplishments" is that I have never felt satisfied with myself. I had a pleasant, occasionally zany adolescence that perhaps one day I might chronicle in a memoir or something, but even on the sunniest summer afternoon or the wildest night with my friends in Greenwich Village, I have never felt *complete*.

All my life, I have wanted nothing more than to achieve. I have wanted to be the "it" girl. But today's "it" girl doesn't "just wanna have fun." In fact, she's probably a little insulted by such an assertion; she wants to work her tail off to exceed others' expectations of her. Today's "it" girl isn't *Clueless*'s flighty heroine Cher—but she has Cher's style and social calendar, with the ambition of Hillary Clinton, the sports skills of Mia Hamm, the wit of Maureen Dowd, and the fake happy endings of a Kate Hudson movie. The "it" girl is pretty, smart, and always in control. At first glance, she's, well, perfect.

The "it" girl isn't the right terminology anymore, though. The "it" girl has too much weight on her shoulders and too many expectations to be a mere mortal. Now, she's a Supergirl. And as I've found out for myself (and as I've seen echoed in the lives of countless of my overachieving peers), this quest for perfection can have a very dark downside.

The stereotypical Supergirl has it all: the good grades, the blossoming career, the impressive activities résumé, the ambitions, and also the good-looking boyfriend, the perfect body, and the impressive social calendar. Supergirls are pigeonholed as young women of elevated socioeconomic status, typically from the suburbs, but who doesn't love a city slicker Supergirl? And the stereotype of the perfection-obsessed Asian or Middle Eastern young women is just as much, if not more, universal than the Supergirl WASP. Says Supergirl Cynthia, a California girl transplanted in Arizona, "I come from a Middle Eastern family and we lived as a strict Catholic household. There were really constant rules: you had to be a lady, you had to perfect, your grades had to be exceptional. Because of this . . . I didn't have my own identity." Supergirls are also stereotyped as discreetly supportive of women's rights and concerned for the world (Supergirls are activists, too!) . . . but they might not be *feminists*, per se.

However, these stereotypes evade the fact that Supergirls are *everywhere*. They are on TV (Ren from *Even Stevens*), they are on the radio (did you know that Hilary Duff sings, acts, diets, volunteers, *and* does venture capitalism?), and they are in the movies (don't even get me started on that actress/Ivy Leaguer/ activist Natalie Portman). They live in homey towns in New Hampshire, the beaches of Florida, the sticks of Missouri, *the* Hills of California, and cities everywhere. But the same facades exist everywhere: these girls aren't particularly happy!

Says Cathy Wasserman, a Brooklyn-based life and career

coach: "This is something that I see in my practice as a psychotherapist and career and executive coach every day, but in the last three to five years, I've seen a significant deepening in this trend. Girls get the message sadly from their own parents and each other that they need to excel at everything, academically, professionally, physically, emotionally, spiritually, and be in perfect balance . . . be a 'perfect 10' in every area. They think that perfection is not only desirable but possible. But this is at odds with our humanity . . . it creates a total impossibility for women."

> "In this climate where women are climbing the corporate ladder more than ever before, all of the sudden, we have this supersexy aesthetic requirement; there's some definite role confusion."
>
> **—Erin, age 26**

And it's this impossibility that keeps young women going: nothing we ever do will be enough! For example, one of my two best friends[2] is a Supergirl. She attends an Ivy League university. She has a GPA of 3.75 in her policy analysis and management program, and earned one of the highest scores in our high school on the SAT. She is very cognizant of politics and is known for thinking before speaking, so every word that comes out of her mouth is cool and insightful. When we were kids, she wrote children's books for fun, and when we were in high school, our English teacher tried to get her to submit her class essays for publication in scholarly journals. Yet she feels slightly unremarkable.

"When you Google me, nothing comes up. I need to have Google prowess. *That's* when I will be successful," she explains to me.

---

2   I will refer to them interchangeably as "my best friend" in this book.

As I think about it, pretty much all my friends fit this mold: they're extremely high-achieving with some combination of great grades, a prestigious college, an impressive job, amazing friends . . . and a steadfast feeling that they're nothing special. I'm fairly certain this has something to do with them being Supergirls.

But this is a little weird. Why are we all working so hard? It isn't just me, it isn't just my family, and it isn't just my friends. It's the girls behind the perfume counters at Macy's and the young woman on line behind you at Starbucks and that awful wretch of a human being who stole your crush and made him her boyfriend. Supergirls are everywhere.

Since When Is Being "Super" a Bad Thing?

On paper, Supergirls look fantastic. When you actually talk to Supergirls, things still look fantastic (after all, all the world's a stage). But when today's young women are really encouraged to open up about the pressures they face, they wholeheartedly reveal that all is not perfect in the realm of perfect girls.

The concept of an overachiever is someone who does something to excess. An achieving girl is one who excels in school or sports or arts, and then makes time for (and values!) hanging out with her friends and family, having hobbies, and sleep. An overachiever isn't like this. An overachiever feels the unremitting requirement not just to be involved, but to be the *best* at every activity at her disposal, and she often feels guilty for penciling in time to relax or even sleep.

This could be written off as just part of what Generation Y is—today's young people do many things to excess. Statistically, we watch a lot of TV, we spend a lot of money (and we all wish we had more money no matter how rich we actually are), we have a lot of sex, we drink a lot, and we devote too much energy to pop culture. And like most of these excesses, working too much is something that is really going to burn us out and hurt us in the long run.

SuEllen Hampkins, coauthor of *The Mother–Daughter Project: How Mothers and Daughters Can Band Together, Beat the Odds, and Survive Through Adolescence*, served as the Smith College psychologist for several years and found that the overwhelming numbers of Supergirls on campus experienced some major issues: "Young women would feel that if they were not simultaneously having exemplary grades, maintaining peak fitness, keeping their weight at a specific slender ideal, and being unfailingly gracious to their friends and family, that they would feel extremely upset with themselves, and that would manifest in all kinds of ways: depression, anxiety, shame, self-hatred."

Says Jessica, a master of divinity candidate at Southern Methodist University in Texas, "Sometimes I have this horrible feeling I am going to let people down, because I really desperately want to make people happy. I don't know if that's just who I am or if it's who I was socialized to be."

Christy, a senior at the University of Washington and longtime Supergirl, is quite conscious of the pressures that drive her. "I've fallen into the overachieving category before where it was about how people viewed me, what society expects of a woman, keeping up with everything from appearance maintenance to pleasing other people to being on time to volunteering. It can be very exhausting for these young women if there's not something that they're passionate about that's driving them, rather than doing all this just to meet the wild expectations of too many people." Christy's working to change the way she was conditioned: she is in therapy and is working her hardest to practice "mindfulness" and live intensely: "I'm working to try to get the joy out of the moment, but it's so easy to get overwhelmed." Christy feels that whether it's being pretty, being sweet, organizing events, or volunteering, "the burden of unpaid and unnoticed work falls upon women . . . it devalues women and it makes women overextended when they have to make a living like everyone else at the same time."

Although Jessica Liebeskind, a celebrity makeup artist who has painted everyone from the Gucci runway models to Nicky Hilton to *The Devil Wears Prada* author Lauren Weisberger, started her own cosmetics company at age 18 and was a top executive at Bobbi Brown Cosmetics by the time she was 22, she doesn't consider herself an overachiever: "I don't know if I qualify as an overachiever. . . . I've just always had this kind of energy. . . . My own conception is that people who are overachievers go above and beyond. I have a friend who is an attorney and a classic overachiever. She did all honors classes in school, and for her, she could only feel like she did 100 percent if she got a 100 on a test and got extra credit . . . the 100 wasn't a 100. She didn't want to be just a cheerleader like I was; she needed to be captain. It wasn't enough to graduate in four years from Stanford; she needed the master's in a four-year program and then needed to go to Yale Law. Just the high levels of things she accomplished would never be good enough. She could never really be satisfied with what she had done."

Clearly, this Supergirl culture can be a real problem. While we should be totally supportive of go-getter young women, we need to be cognizant of the girls whose assiduousness becomes an obsession, where 100 isn't good enough, and overachieving eventually becomes an addiction. Or a mental disorder.

What's troubling, though, is that the young women who have more opportunities than ever before feel so suffocated . . . and they can't pinpoint where this hyperactivity sprouts from! I had always claimed that my Supergirl-ism was due to the fact that I never enjoyed mundane teenage schedules like entire weekends spent getting drunk, recovering from a hangover in bed all day, browsing celebrity blogs, and doing it all over again. The reality? I'd never actually tried it: my life always had a to-do list. Ever since I was an adolescent, I had an agenda: achieve something.

I suffered from eating disorders as a teen (anorexia, exercise bulimia, and overeating), and I always thought that it just screwed me up. But when I had totally candid conversations with my friends and other young women, I realized it's not just me. Totally healthy girls with no history of mental disorders were perfection-obsessed girls. It had to come from somewhere else.

In her book, *The Overachievers: The Secret Lives of Driven Kids,* Yale grad and recovering overachiever Alexandra Robbins studied the immense pressure on high schoolers to get into good colleges. She writes, "When teenagers inevitably look at themselves through the prism of our overachiever culture, they often come to the conclusion that no matter how much they achieve, it will never be enough."

And this is exactly what is going on with the Supergirl dilemma, except that it's more trying for women. Students—male or female—who bust their butts in high school, popping study drugs and pulling all-nighters, know that there are hard measures of whether they've "succeeded," like grades, SAT scores, and whether they finally get into Penn State or Amherst. But for young women, there is no rubric for being smart enough, accomplished enough, or thin enough; young women don't know if they've completed all their goals to the extreme until they're— not to be morbid—in the hospital for exhaustion.

We are quick to congratulate—or even envy—a young

woman who wakes up at five in the morning to go jogging before spending all day in AP classes at school, then leading a school newspaper meeting, then going to lacrosse practice, then making a cameo at her boyfriend's basketball game, before studying and finally retiring to bed. On the surface, this appears to be progress for young women—instead of being ousted from honors chemistry classes by their male counterparts or harboring fallacies of how romantic it would be to vacuum in high heels on Wisteria Lane for the rest of their lives, young women are busting through the glass ceiling faster than you can say "overachiever."

But this isn't necessarily progress for women. Today's Supergirls, the young women who juggle earning perfect grades, leading youth organizations, trying to make their families proud, trekking down their career paths years ahead of schedule (and trying to make it look like a happenstance trajectory), maintaining perfect figures, and entertaining cute boyfriends (although more often it's more for validation than for the affection of having a boyfriend—it's not wanting arm candy, it's *being* arm candy) without releasing a single bead of sweat, aren't what they seem. These Supergirls are, more often than not, deeply unsatisfied with their lives. While it's normal to admire these assiduous young women, their Spartan efforts are often rooted in self-dissatisfaction. Young women have been trained not to feel good about themselves, no matter what they do. These young women running on less than four hours of sleep a night (and fourteen hundred calories a day) aren't Herculean: young women are dying for the validation and approval that society has historically denied them.

If we didn't explore this—that the Supergirl dilemma is tied directly to sexism and societal misogyny—then perhaps the most peculiar thing about Supergirls would be that they have no *concrete* reason to work to the point of disease. With the exception of girls on academic scholarships who need to work hard to keep their GPAs up to earn or retain scholarships, all of the young women I've spoken to weren't seeking mobility or freedom through their working; they were seeking validation. In my experience, Supergirls generally aren't working fourteen hours a day to feed their families or to get out of the welfare system; on some level, their stressing is pretty superfluous. If a young woman in an immigrant family needed to juggle school and activities and an after-school job so that she could get a scholarship to college and help her family pay bills, it would make sense. But for upper-middle-class girls who are spending sixty hours a week working toward some amorphous success, the Supergirl dilemma is more a reflection of how the status of women and girls isn't doing so hot. Young women have been taught to find themselves in being perfect . . . but given that those feelings of *meaning something* can only come from inside, they're going to be looking for a while.

> "There are a lot of rules for girls and girls' behavior today."
>
> **—Gina, age 15**

Look Deeper

In elementary school, one of my teachers told us on the first day of class after holiday vacation to brainstorm some New Year's resolutions. One of the girls in my class, a pretty, popular girl with sleek brown hair and a pearly smile, shared hers with the class:

"I want to be good."

Our teacher was a smart, savvy woman who pressed my classmate:

"What do you mean by 'good'? Is 'good' studying hard in

school? Is 'good' having nice friends? Or is it being nice to your siblings?"

The girl blushed and said, "I don't know. . . ."

Seven or eight years later, she graduated from high school with flattering senior superlatives, honors, and an acceptance letter to a good school. However, she had also dealt with eating disorders, clique crap, and periodic breakdowns at her locker.

Today's young women have been taught to be "good." From playing in the sandbox to smiling in prom and graduation pictures to unveiling a work presentation in the boardroom, being good has been the main objective. But what does good mean? Does it mean being a good daughter? Does it mean acting like a lady? Does it mean not making others angry? Does it mean being pretty and skinny? Does it mean joining the "it" sorority? Does it mean being passive? Does it mean not having sex? Does it mean having sex (but only to please guys)?

Because no one knows what parents (and, essentially, what society) mean when they tell girls to be good, girls assume that being good means doing everything—and doing everything right. Today's young women have essentially been cultivated to be perfect, yet they don't have a clear definition of what this means or how to achieve it. It's something I've been struggling with my whole life. So I decided to look into it for myself—I proposed to investigate this Supergirl phenomenon from the inside, not as a dispassionate observer, but as one of the Supergirls.

For my reporting on this topic, I've traveled to high schools, colleges, and offices around the country to report on the state of the Supergirl. I've sat in on classes and club meetings, eavesdropped on conversations, crashed lunch dates, and, plainly, observed. I've combined this firsthand reportage with countless expert interviews (talking with authors and researchers who are studying these high-flying superachievers) and conversations with dozens of Supergirls themselves, some of whom you'll get to know rather well through these pages. I have done my best to reflect racial, geographical, and socioeconomic diversity in the Supergirls whose opinions I've included and whose thoughts I've shared.

However, the main characters who you will meet, and who I hope you will see yourself in, represent the diversity of the Supergirl dilemma. They span from being lower middle class to upper middle class; they represent various races and ethnicities, geographies (they live and have lived everywhere from Alaska to Georgia to New York to Austria to Canada, in large cities and rural towns), and political viewpoints; and they span in age from 15 to 27. They reflect varying degrees of Supergirl behavior and each views their lifestyles differently, although what they have in common are their high goals, high hopes for the future, and determined work ethic.

What's another thing that today's young women have in common? They're incredible. They are just as good as the guys and they know it. However, although it's no longer *en vogue* to call young women Ophelias, I think they are still facing many of the pressures as described in Dr. Mary Pipher's 1999 bestselling *Reviving Ophelia: Saving the Selves of Adolescent Girls*. But today's Supergirls lattice their pain with acceptance letters to prestigious colleges, expensive foundation from Sephora, and blue ribbons, so it looks like progress.

I have a feeling that the self-actualization that people require cannot come from SAT scores or thinness or having it all. I've found that when my friends and I tell ourselves, "We'll be ___ enough when we're ___," we're not doing whatever it is for the right reasons . . . and we probably won't end up satisfied when we achieve our goal.

So let's go down the yellow brick road of overachieving and explore where this dissatisfaction comes from.

chapter two

"I'm So Old!"

Supergirls Achieve Early . . .
But It's Never Enough

....

Pepsi . . . for those who think young!
—Britney Spears in a 2002 Pepsi-Cola commercial

Today's high schoolers possess schedules similar to the ones that 30-year-olds work around. They get minimal sleep in favor of running around from obligation to obligation and stressing out over what hasn't been done or what could be done. And they expect themselves to not only do more and to do it better, but also to accomplish it *earlier.*

In a culture where young people are becoming more and more accomplished, age is the standard that success is often measured against. After all, how often do we hear someone say, "So-and-so has accomplished x, y, and z, and she is only q years old!" Which puts more and more pressure on young people to achieve and makes them feel old when they don't overachieve.

Being a teenage girl is no longer about "sugar, spice, and

everything nice." It's about being the pretty girl in high heels who looks harmless but surprises everyone with getting top scores on the SAT and using words like *exculpate, compendium,* and *circumlocution* without them sounding forced. Supergirls in high school (and sometimes even middle school!) have a lot on their plates: the pressure to get into a good college through good grades and participation in lots of activities starts early, the pressure to be popular and well liked starts even earlier, and the pressure to please everyone is almost completely engrained in childhood.

Pegah, Age 15, Valley Stream North High School

My mom, who grew up in Nassau County, New York, said that back in her day, North High School "had all the cute boys." And though it's about thirty years later when I visit Pegah one fall day at North High School, the scene feels positively time-less. It's Friday and tomorrow the school is playing their archri-val in football, so beefy 17-year-old guys hulk down the halls in their white jerseys; the cheerleaders have each asked a football player to lend them their spare green jerseys, which the girls wear like billowy tunics tucked into their short cheerleading skirts.

The rest of the engaged percentage of the student body that isn't getting ready for the game still practices some form of school spirit. Highly ambitious girls who participate in clubs and chair student government committees flit by in miniskirts and low-riders that sweep the floor despite the high heels on these girls; their male counterparts don't seem as engaged, chilling out in front of their lockers and being part of the high school foliage rather than zipping along to their next classes.

Pegah, a very pretty sophomore of Iranian descent, got

slighted in one of the worst ways a high school can slight some-one: she was assigned the bottom locker in the stacks of two lockers that line the hallways. Lucky for her, her things are meticulously organized, so when she crouches to get her English materials, she brushes her long brown hair out of her face, quickly grabs the right books and binders, and is good to go. Her entourage of 15-year-old friends, each girl meticulously groomed and pretty, surrounds her, gabbing about the game tomorrow and the antics going on in biology and OMG *did you hear about blah, blah, blah?*

Pegah, who is a small girl, weaves through the crowds in the halls effortlessly, her friends following her and filing into their English class. Pegah has her binder for the class out and is flipping through her perfectly organized papers when the final bell rings; she smiles to a few acquaintances and sits up straight at her desk. The students are working on a practice test for the Regents exams, New York State's standardized tests that are used to measure students' aptitude in subjects like biology, chemistry, American history, French, and English, among many others. It is to be noted, however, that as Pegah and her peers peruse passages about forest fires and answer corresponding questions to assess comprehension, the exam they are prepping for isn't until the end of their junior year, in approximately nineteen months.

"This is really hard," concedes Pegah's teacher, a younger woman in a denim skirt and creamsicle-colored cardigan. "I didn't have the key when I first tried this practice test, and I actually got three wrong."

Later, Pegah admitted, only a touch gleefully, that she only got one question wrong.

Virtually all of the eight classes Pegah is taking in school are honors, advanced placement (AP), or part of an accelerated track where she enters courses meant for students at least a year or so older than her. She has a tight-knit group of friends who are cheerleaders, smart kids, members of student government, and athletes; she identifies every single one of them as a perfectionist.

Pegah's next class, AP European history, is one that comes with a little bit of hard feelings: "The teacher came into my history class last year and was really intimidating and told us all about how much work her class would be and how if we wanted to do AP Euro, we had to be really serious, and she was frankly, kind of scary." So, when Pegah got her summer assignment, which was composed of some readings, some worksheets, and seven questions that could be answered from the readings, Pegah took her teacher's stern greeting to heart. Pegah wrote thirty-six pages for the seven questions: "It took me literally all summer. And because I had the entire summer to do it, I always felt like I could put more time into it . . . so I did." The worst part? The teacher didn't even collect it. Not to mention, when her teacher registered the expanse of Pegah's work, "She sort of turned up her nose and was like, 'I really only wanted a paragraph for each question. I wouldn't want to have to grade all that.' I wrote five pages for each question . . . essentially a research paper!" Although Pegah didn't say anything or outwardly appear angry, she admits, "I had to leave the room. I wanted to swear and scream *soooo bad*! That assignment was my *summer*."

Now it's November, and Pegah sits in the left corner of the front row of her AP Euro class answering the questions that are written on the blackboard. Students are supposed to write the answers first thing when they enter the classroom, and Pegah seems to regurgitate the answers effortlessly. But just because she's good at the class doesn't cool the tensions that she spent the entire summer slaving over an unnecessary school assignment.

Pegah concedes that she's not actually bitchy; instead, she recognizes that female power in ninety-pound packages is often hard for others to swallow without bottling it as something loathsome like bitchiness. I'd also be willing to gamble that her status as a minority student gives other students automatic conceptions about her personality and approach to school.

However, what's heartening about the school is that, for a mostly white suburb of New York City where the driveways of raised ranches all have at least two nice cars in them and local tanning salons offer stand-up booths for $2/minute, the racial and (presumably) economic diversity of the school is wide-ranging. The Supergirl dilemma is stereotyped as a phenomenon among the white upper classes—and this is more often than not true—but it seems that there is a strong push to get all the students at Pegah's school involved in AP classes. It did appear to be the polished girls with Tiffany jewelry jangling on their wrists dying to answer questions in class, but often the teachers would nod and acknowledge their enthusiasm, then prompt the quieter students—who sometimes were the poorer-looking boys or the black kids—to participate and offer their opinions and feedback. There is obviously going to be some hard feelings about focusing on a phenomenon that seems to flower among relatively privileged girls; after all, the average household in Valley Stream, New York, has a total income between $75,000 and $100,000.

What's hard to swallow in hearing Pegah and watching her, however, is that she is only 15! Here is a girl who gets home from school around 3:30, studies until dinner, then studies until it's time to shower and pick out her clothes for the next day, and then studies until she passes out: "I don't like to watch TV before bed because my friend told me that you forget like 40 percent of everything that you learned because the TV waves do something to your brain, I don't know." Which is a shame, because TV is a very cathartic factor for Pegah; after finals week this past June, she stayed in bed for two days and watched TV to ease the stress of having essentially worked ninety-hour weeks studying and taking tests for the preceding month: "But then I got sick of it after the first day and a half. Relaxing is not one of the things I do well."

Katie, Age 17, Syracuse University's School Press Institute

Syracuse University's campus in central New York is centered around a grassy quad lined with ivy-covered brick buildings that house some of the country's best academic programs in engineering, law, and communications. On nearby streets stand regal rows of fraternity and sorority houses with immaculate gardens and big Greek letters nailed to the top of the houses. The rest of the campus is towered over by castle-like buildings on steep hills that look transplanted from *Harry Potter* and *The Addams Family*.

During the school year, students swarm around the lively campus from classes to study groups to soccer games to parties, which have given the school the reputation of being for incredibly intelligent people who work hard, play hard, and grow up to make more money than 90 percent of the population. During the winter, the campus is blanketed in snow like thick, sugary frosting on a child's birthday cake, so students strive to stay inside to study, party, and watch Syracuse basketball games on TV. During the summer, it is hot as hell, and every July, high school students from around the country come to the Syracuse campus to attend the School Press Institute (SPI), an intensive journalism camp for students to learn and refine their skills in writing, photography, newspaper layout, video journalism, leading a newspaper staff, and yearbook editing. I attended SPI the summer before my sophomore year of high school, and it was a really important experience for me: having just recovered from a year of eating disorders and put on a lot of weight, I was able to go and make friends and realize that I was still likable, *and* it made me realize, for certain, that I wanted to become a journalist.

In the summer of 2007, I get to go again, this time as an observer.

While moms, dads, and nervous-looking teenagers pour out of streams of black SUVs and blue minivans clutching stand-up fans, desk lamps, and duffle bags, I park my own car to hang out for a week with one of the largest gatherings of Supergirls I've ever seen.

Kids who go to academic summer camps already have their maturity vouched for them. They pass up summer days of sitting on the couch watching MTV, eating Doritos for breakfast at 11am, and drinking cans of beer in the woods at night to sit in classrooms, do homework, and learn. However, even at the first class I attend, the students I meet amaze me.

Katie, a pretty girl with fair skin, shiny brown hair, and girl-next-door appeal, who is from a small town in western New York, befriends me in class. She is the youngest of three children and lives at home with her mom and dad, who she is very close with, especially because they lived in a remote part of Alaska for some time when Katie was growing up. She's a rising high school senior, and devoutly Christian, hoping to go to a Baptist college in Pennsylvania. Her list of extracurricular activities is impressive, but what's more telling is that she is an administrative assistant for her older sister's start-up company, babysits pro bono for said sister's kids, and helps her parents with their catering company . . . she's the perfect daughter.

In class we're having a sort of mock editorial meeting where the students, who were just working in pairs to brainstorm ideas, are bouncing story ideas off one another and discussing broader issues in Generation Y that apply to their school that they could localize and write about in their school papers.

Katie, who had been working with her friend Stephanie, a dark-haired Supergirl who is an amateur ballerina and the incoming editor-in-chief of their school newspaper, came up with a pretty alarming story idea: "We want to write about kids abusing energy drinks," Katie told the class. "Because there are lots of kids in our school who have four or five Red Bulls during a school day. Like, they will have one in the morning to wake up, and then they'll have to keep drinking them to fend off the crash that you get an hour after finishing a Red Bull."

This initially strikes me as something you'd hear about among investment bankers on Wall Street, given the stereotypes that investment bankers guzzle black eyes (three shots of espresso in a venti coffee) or do lines of cocaine and then handle millions of dollars of mergers and acquisitions in a manic frenzy before passing out at their desks or starting the cycle again. But I can't imagine that high schoolers would be so obsessed with their school day—or feel so burdened by the expectations on them—so as to ingest really dangerous and unhealthy quantities of caffeine to get through AP U.S. history. However, another girl jumps in and says, "We just did a piece sort of like this for our school newspaper, because a lot of kids were drinking Cocaine, that new energy drink that was taken off the market because it was so strong—and I think people had a problem with the name—so there was this sort of underground operation to get your hands on Cocaine."

"Kids at my school don't drink Cocaine," says a delicate blonde girl, who appears to be repressing a smirk after uttering the name of the taboo drug. "But kids at my school do chain-drink Vitamin Water. You walk by the garbage cans and they are overflowing with empty Vitamin Water bottles . . . especially the energy flavor. And even though that's not as extreme, it's still bad, because you can unknowingly consume a lot of caffeine."

Katie nods in agreement and continues: "Our school newspaper actually already did a story sort of like the one that I'm proposing—maybe this could be a follow-up feature or something—because there's this Web site where you can calculate how many Red Bulls you have to drink to kill you, and we feel like that's really representative of the intensity that people our age are consuming caffeine. But we didn't put the name of the Web site in the paper because we were afraid that kids would calculate how many they had to drink—based on their gender and weight and stuff—and then actually try it." (I Googled "death by energy drink calculator" later that day and learned that it would take almost one hundred Red Bulls to kill the average teen girl . . . but anyone who has ever sampled the neon yellow energy drink knows that it only takes two Red Bulls to make you shake and three to make you feel really, really sick. Throw vodka into the mix and you're up for a tumultuous ride.)

Clearly, there is some sort of unhealthy dynamic in high schools of having to act much older than you actually are and having responsibilities and pressures that require you to guzzle energy drinks . . . and still being a young person, potentially reckless enough to consume a fatal quantity of energy drinks.

Katie and her friends and I go out to dinner between the afternoon and evening classes at a diner on a quaint street of shops in town. While we order pizza and eggplant parmesan heroes, Katie has to sneak out and buy a wheat bagel from the Dunkin' Donuts down the street.

"That's how she stays so skinny," Katie's friend says to me. "She's allergic to, like, white flour and dairy and sugar and, well, pretty much everything except for fruit, some meat, and wheat bread. So, like when she wants to eat junk, she can't because she doesn't have a choice. I wish I had food allergies!"

Katie comes back and discreetly eats her smuggled wheat bagel, and I feel sorry for her to have to be 17 and have to worry so much about her diet . . . but she seems, more than anything, thankful that's she's "not so ill all the time" like she was before she learned she had food allergies. In fact, she doesn't so much as glance at anyone eating pizza.

"Hey, what exactly is your book about?" Katie's friend asks me.

"It's about the girls who want to do it all, like balancing school and work and activities and getting into college and being pretty, without looking stressed out."

"Something we all deal with," she says and smiles.

"You think it's that pervasive?" I ask.

"Of course," another one of the girls chimes in and smiles.

However, the girls don't appear *that* burdened. While this could have been because it was summer and beautiful outside, at one of the country's most elite college campuses, given that few people were sleeping more than five hours a night, there was definitely some "acting" going on.

"I'm so tired I could punch someone," Katie's friend Deanna commented one morning. "But, you know, I'm keeping it to myself."

And these girls have some grown-up worries. As 16-year-olds, they're grappling with the cost of college, not getting stabbed at sports games, and working so hard and having every hour of their days accounted for in clubs and classes and homework and workouts . . . so what happened to childhood? And when life is this much in fast forward, won't these kids be graying by the time they're 25?

Lots of Pressure

I decided in high school, at age 15, that I wanted to have published a book by the time I was 18 and attend a very well-known college. Neither of these goals were accomplished—I am 18 years old as I am writing this chapter. I will be 20 when this book is published. I am attending a perfectly good (if not Ivy League) university. And despite everything, I am strangely embarrassed about my age and what I've accomplished so far. I feel like I haven't yet done enough.

I know that I'm not the only fairly accomplished young woman who feels frustrated with herself: when Supergirls set unattainable goals for themselves (and perhaps attach an age to the goal), if they do not achieve this goal or if the age they assigned to this goal comes and goes without the goal, they start to feel old. And this self-imposed pressure begins in high school (or even earlier).

I went to a seventh- through twelfth-grade high school, from 2000 to 2005 (I spent my senior year taking classes at the local community college as part of an acceleration program); the school was small, with a little more than a hundred twenty kids in a grade, most of whom dressed the same, talked the same, had similar family incomes, and all wanted to go to a college that people had heard of. As such, to my surprise, high school turned out to be nothing like what I saw in teen movies. Students actually did homework . . . a lot of homework! And clubs, sports, community service, and outside activities! The dumb guys who started fights, wore too much Axe body spray, and didn't push themselves academically were somewhat shunned; while there was still a push for girls to diminish their intelligence, being a "ditzy girl" was also somewhat looked down upon. There was a high premium put on broadcasting a calm, cool, collected image:

wearing Ralph Lauren and Abercrombie, working constantly, and not going against the grain were highly rewarded in our social culture. While I definitely didn't go to a Stepford school (senior pranks were of utmost importance), my school did seem to be somewhat of a hothouse for high-anxiety high achievers . . . especially among girls.

There were too many Supergirls to name: perhaps thirty or more in every grade, meaning that at least half the female population was Supergirls. There was definitely an air of girls trying to be effortlessly perfect, striding out of AP classes in khaki miniskirts and navy blue Abercrombie sweaters, swishing their glossy straight hair over their shoulders carrying test papers with red 95's on the top . . . and making it look as though it were all easy. Except, we all knew it wasn't easy, but no one wanted to bring it up. Whining was fairly usual—*"Can you believe how much homework there is in AP U.S.?"* or, *"Ugh . . . I can't believe I don't have a lunch or study hall this year,"* and, of course, *"I'm tired and it is so freezing in this #*$&-ing school"*—but there was never a hint of actually being put out by or wanting to challenge the unreasonable hours of AP U.S. homework or an inclination to skip a newspaper meeting and take a nap, because that would mean not maximizing in this rubric of stereotypical high school success.

I soon learned that these attitudes weren't unique to my high school.

"I have no life outside of school," explains Liz, a 17-year-old from Revere High School in Massachusetts. "It's a scheduling problem—no one has time. If you wanted to put your all into classes and into all the activities you take on, it would be very easy to not sleep."

"I don't really need that much sleep," says Erika, a public high school sophomore from western New York. Erika, who competes in horse riding and equestrian shows, has a severe challenge to balance her dedication to fitness and her demanding school schedule with honors classes, club meetings, and sports practices. "I wake up at 4:30am to go to the barn, where I work before school on Wednesdays, Thursdays, and Fridays. Then I try to fit in a two- or three-mile run before showering, getting ready for school, and being in school until three. I take really hard classes and the teachers demand a lot of you, and sometimes I need to actively work to not show that I'm kind of exhausted and freaking out during the day."

Being in an all-girls' environment changes the tone a bit: "Going to an all-girls' high school really made me into a powerful woman," says Samantha, now a sophomore at NYU. Samantha grew up on a cranberry bog (which I think is just fascinating), and she became the queen of the overachievers at an exclusive girls' boarding school in Massachusetts.

Samantha—almost literally—was a member of nearly every club available and served in some kind of leadership position within each. She also rewrote the student handbook as a project during her senior year to cultivate a more harmonious student body ("Girls were always stealing each other's Coach bags, which is ridiculous when your dad is a millionaire and girls' schools are supposed to be about sisterhood"). Only Samantha had a bit of a secret: doing all of this wasn't nearly as effortless as it seemed.

"By my junior year I was really tired and I didn't want anyone to know I was tired, so the constant acting was even more exhausting. . . . I was also really struggling with my sexuality, and by the time I was a senior, I had an eating disorder . . . and no one knew that I was having a hard time and that doing all this stuff was really hard. . . . I was having this huge struggle and budding epiphany about who I was and what I was passionate about, but the amount of work and expectations on me prevented me from working this through and writing and being able to think clearly about what was going on. And if high school is all about growing and becoming an adult, then why wasn't my self-reflecting considered as important as my studying and clubs?"

The high school extracurricular scene is a huge source of overextension. Young people are encouraged to join as many clubs as they can fit into their schedules . . . but it doesn't breed genuine young people. In fact, the way that students are encouraged by teachers, peers, and college admissions people to be in five or more clubs that could be totally unrelated to their interests not only takes up time, but it also teaches young people that halfhearted attempts at participation in boring stuff earns brownie points.

"It's hard because, like, I focus on my schoolwork, so I'm up until 12 at night working and I have to be at school at 7:30, but I still have to take care of stereotypical girl things, like making sure that I look halfway decent to go to school, especially because everyone in my town is so affluent that everyone is dressed nicely."

—**Allison, age 17**

The *New York Times* ran a cover story on "amazing girls" in April 2007, focusing on a Supergirl, Esther Mobley (and her Supergirl friends!), who attended high school in a suburb of Boston. While the author of this article, "For Girls, It's Be Yourself, and Be Perfect, Too," framed the Supergirl discussion through the lens of Supergirls being immune to insecurity, eating disorders, and internal crises, which obviously isn't true, the article did discuss the concept of overextension through extracurricular activities:

"You're supposed to have all these extracurriculars, to play sports and do theater," said another of Esther's 17-year-old classmates, Julie Mhlaba, who aspires to medical school and juggles three Advanced Placement classes, gospel choir and a part-time job as a waitress. "You're supposed to do well in your classes and still have time to go out." . . .

Jennifer Price, the Newton North principal, said she and her faculty emphasized to students that they could win admission to many excellent colleges without organizing their entire lives around résumé building. By age 14, Ms. Price said, the school's highest fliers are already worrying about marketing themselves to colleges: "You almost have to be superhuman to resist the pressure."

The Supergirls I met who scurried between student government meetings, Spanish club meetings, debate team practice, theater rehearsals, and environmental club meetings—who wanted to be engineers or accountants—seemed to see their involvement in these clubs more as obligations than opportunities for enrichment. Whereas the girls in this same combination of clubs who wanted to be foreign political consultants or documentary directors actually seemed to *like* what they did after school . . . but these girls were few and far between. I don't think anyone (outside of Newton North's principal) ever expressly told today's young adults that clubs are for them to dabble in various academic concentrations and hone their interests . . . and that authenticity is *really* important!

Unrealistic Expectations

When I think of high school, the first thing I think of is lockers slamming, girls in cashmere sweaters and miniskirts walking away with brown lunch bags in their hands, and boys in khaki pants and navy blue sweaters feverishly copying one another's homework against the lockers. I think of people focusing on pop quizzes and college admissions by day, and parties and hookups by night.

And the problem is that these thought processes are actually really damaging. "It would be so much easier if our society allowed for adolescence and high school to be the awkward, uneasy, unsure time of change that it really is, because young people could really be comfortable," says Marisa Meltzer, a teen magazine freelancer and author of *How* Sassy *Changed My Life: A Love Letter to the Greatest Teen Magazine of All Time*. "Instead, we have this MTV-inspired idea that young people need to be pretty and graceful, and I think that really fuels the problem."

I think these unrealistic expectations about high school fuel the Supergirl myth. Although I met girls as young as 11 who demonstrated Supergirl characteristics, many young women destined to be Supergirls seem to begin fulfilling the role when they enter high school, and I think it's largely because the teen media—television, magazines, movies—devotes a lot of time to glamorizing the pretty, smart, well-liked, multitasking teen girls who do it all. Correspondingly, high school systems spend a lot of time and energy lauding the school Supergirls. At the end of every year, my high school had awards ceremonies, giving everyone the opportunity to see who the high-achieving students were. While the good thing is that it was no longer cool to be the moody cheerleader who smoked cigarettes in the bathroom, these ceremonies discreetly taught kids that achievement is always judged by someone else's standards. This, in combination with teachers giving too much homework, the girls on magazine covers getting skinnier, and newspapers constantly running articles about how increasingly difficult it is to get into college, gives young women the message that nothing they do is enough.

Jessica, a Supergirl and vocal feminist, grew up in Arkansas, where girls learned early on that it's good to be smart, better to be hot, and best to be both . . . as long as you're not *too* smart. "My high school was so cutthroat—it was straight out of *Mean Girls*," Jessica says in her sweet Southern twang. "The ideal girl was on drill team, she was in the band, and she was a wonderful student . . . but the things she 'put on her wall,' the things she invested herself in were always things that emphasized her grace and beauty rather than her intellect." Jessica feels that this is because her old-fashioned community valued beauty in girls more than smarts . . . and girls were getting a lot of mixed messages. "I would try to downplay my academic achievements. I don't think I ever really wanted to go to any of the awards presentations or banquets I was invited to. . . . My family always encouraged my achieving, but at school it was totally different. You wanted to be pretty over everything. I wish I could talk to the fifteen-year-old me and tell her that it's actually better to be smart."

I've always had a beef with the pressures on girls in high school, but it's hard to hold anyone accountable for it, because high school is a huge locale of socialization. High school is the watering hole, the martini shaker, and the microcosm of the "real world" where all of young people's influences are welded together. It's as though Judy McGrath (CEO of MTV), Mom, Dad, George Bush, Hillary Clinton, Britney Spears, and your best friend all share a lunch table.

Finally, the privilege issue is a huge contributor to the presence of Supergirls in high schools. In the *New York Times* article on amazing girls, the reporter noted that the average home in the community where she did her research cost $750,000 and the Supergirl she shadowed wore True Religion jeans (which retail in boutiques for around $300) to school. The rise of shows like *My Super Sweet Sixteen* and *The Hills* has created a culture where people know about the luxuries of the social classes several rungs above them and makes even the wealthiest teens feel underprivileged. And it figures into this culture of wanting perfectly: of wanting better grades, better SAT scores, and a brand-name college. . . .

However, this mindset of adoring the privileged creates its own myths. There is this concept that the girls in the expensive private schools and the richest communities are the most troubled; they experience the most pressure to be perfect. But in my research I found that young women of *all* socioeconomic statuses experience this pressure, especially the lower-class girls who were conditioned to covet the toys and baubles of those of the upper classes and know that perhaps they could create lives like that for their children if they worked really hard. "My high school is rough," says Liz of Revere, Massachusetts. "And I do think that a lot of the kids who work so hard are working for social mobility."

Without getting into the public versus private debate, the most important thing high schools can do to help their students is teach them to be genuine. Given that young people are taught to change who they are and portray themselves in a way that contrasts with their authenticity—in social situations, in job interviews, on college applications—a sense of "it's okay to be you" is hugely important. After all, with the college admissions process coming up, they're going to need it.

The College Admissions Rat Race

I got rejected from Barnard College, the women's college of Columbia University. And as far as I was concerned, my life was over.

This was partly because the rejection totally threw a wrench in my plan to attend a prestigious college in Manhattan and date a cute blue-blood Columbia boy (and also squelched my more serious plans to live in New York City to network, intern, and meet others who knew ways to make my secret dream of becoming a playwright and screenwriter a lucrative reality). But I was also crushed because it affirmed all my suspicions about the college admissions process and Supergirls.

"The college admissions process takes you down a notch in the first place," says Rachel, a high school senior from upstate New York, "because you have to write down all your accomplishments on a few pages and you look at it and say, 'These are the material things I've done with the past four years.' Then you start hearing about other kids who have a whole page more of activities and accomplishments than you, and even though maybe you had different ways of evaluating yourself and looking at your success, you start to feel smaller; the college admissions process lines people up and literally compares them."

"As an educator, what's disappointing is that the way the college admissions process is currently set up, it requires perfection," says Trudy Hall, the head of the Emma Willard School in Troy, New York. "A girl really can't have an 'off' month or get a B in social studies sophomore year if she wants to go to Middlebury or what have you. That grade alone would knock her out of the running."

Says Allison, a Supergirl entering her junior year at Guilderland High School in upstate New York, "It's so hard to get into the best colleges because everyone has to make themselves look better than everyone else, and as everyone is doing more things to get ahead, everyone else has to do more and more to look attractive to colleges in return. It's like the formula to get into college is simply, *spread yourself too thin*."

"I wish there was just a set formula for kids to get into college, like, 'If you want to go to Dartmouth, if you have exactly this, you can get in,'" says Jared Friebel, an English teacher at Hinsdale High School, a prestigious public school in a suburb of Chicago. "Because then I think students would be so much less stressed and anxious. They're sort of walking on eggshells for the last two years of high school hoping that whatever they do will work out and get them to a good school."

> "I have no life outside of school."
> **—Liz, age 17**

But when this manic overextension doesn't come through and a Supergirl finds that a college isn't impressed, a college rejection for a Supergirl kills. Every day, from the moment they wake up to the second they pass out twenty hours later, Supergirls are telling themselves that they could do more. This is, however, with the latent understanding that they *are* doing enough; every Supergirl blushes and burrows her cheek into her shoulder when she is reminded by others of how accomplished she is, because she knows it's a little true. So for a college that a Supergirl liked enough to spend her precious time completing an application to reject her is substantiating her worst fears about herself.

While college rejection letters are worded in a cutesy way, delicately relating the record number of increasingly qualified applicants, they basically tell you that you weren't good enough. And it kills, especially because Supergirls are so goal oriented that all year, as they are prying their eyes open at five in the morning to study more, shower, and get to school, they are carroting themselves with their image at their desired college campuses.

So, I got rejected from Barnard. And my life seemed over . . . for a day or two (okay, fine a month). But, as Laura

Jeanne Hammond, editor of *Next Step* magazine puts it, "A rejection from a college is actually a blessing in disguise. The college admissions people know their campus best, and by rejecting students, they are steering kids who wouldn't fit in at the school to places where they will be better suited."

Samantha, the head girl at the Dana Hall School, had an unnerving experience with her college applications. She had trouble with the concept that schools only cared about her SAT scores and the grades on her transcript: "It felt like they wanted these concrete yet very superficial measures of who I was." So, in a completely un-Supergirl-esque move, Samantha turned down admissions offers to several prestigious colleges (and stomached painful rejections from a few prestigious schools) and instead got her chance to have an unobstructed transformation period while doing community service in Washington, D.C., for a year with City Year, a branch of Americorps.

"No one that I worked with at City Year cared that I went to a swanky high school and had all these accomplishments. They liked me because I was *me*. . . . The high-pressure nature of high school completely distracted me from being able to figure out who I wanted to be, but when I got away from the expectations and people wanting me to act a certain way, I was able to really learn about who I was."

In Fast Forward

Our society is obsessed with youth, and it makes people do and feel crazy things: 40-something mothers wear low-rider jeans and 50-something dads feel compelled to watch MTV. Television producers create unrealistic depictions of young people in slightly scripted, highly sensationalized "reality" television shows.

And 18-year-old Supergirls feel old. It sounds completely crazy, but it actually makes sense—in a culture where young people are becoming more and more accomplished, age is the standard that achievement is measured against.

And it's not just accomplishment that is coming earlier to us. I have several friends who are my age and slightly older who discuss the chronology of their lives in terms of before and after "getting sober."[1] The year after I graduated high school, I found out that students in the grades below me had taken to cocaine and lounging in the VIP rooms of Albany bars. While it would be hugely naive of me to assume that Generation Y is the first cohort of kids to take to drugs and alcohol at a young age, the rationale for doing so is very different. Our parents did acid at Grateful Dead concerts because they were creating a revolution in the middle class! But today's young people use drugs and alcohol to escape; an entire "big red cup" of wine or a line of cocaine can—however ephemerally—make kids forget almost entirely about the perceived boredom and anxiety of being middle class.

Our generation's obsession with privilege has also aged us greatly. Other generations probably had no clue about the toys and luxuries adorning the social classes well above them, whereas when children watch Mary-Kate and Ashley Olsen movies where the girls sleep in ornately decorated bedrooms in Paris and preteen girls read in magazines about Hilary Duff's obsession with shopping, we have a recipe for disaster at worst and constant discontent at best. Children learn in Sunday school that coveting is bad, but they're taught how to do it as soon as they watch *High School Musical 2,* where Ashley Tisdale sings, "Fetch me my Jimmy Choo flip-flops. Where is my pink Prada tote? I need my Tiffany hairband. . . !"

---

1   Although these periods of sobriety tend to last around three days to two weeks.

I would argue that media and the stimulation overload in Generation Y-ers' lives age them. Never before have young people been so engulfed in the media: news tickers are installed in many high schools and on college campuses; televisions are installed everywhere from the waiting rooms of academic advising offices in colleges to the backseats of taxis. There are even televisions in the individual examination rooms of my dentist's office . . . which is actually pretty cool but also very problematic. After all, there isn't that much media that is intended to teach people, *You are good the way you are! You don't need extra stuff to feel complete! Being middle class is great!* The concept of media and advertising is to teach people, *Hey, your life would be a little cooler if you had the new iPod or if you watched the Thursday night lineup on the CW, where you'll learn more about how lame your life is.*

But this isn't what childhood and adolescence are supposed to be. Childhood is supposed to be innocent, fun, careless!

Here's the thing: I already regret not appreciating my childhood and adolescence more. I spent so much time in high school wanting to be "grown up" that I bought business cards and professional outfits, *dying* for a chance to use them. I wanted so badly for someone other than my friends to call my cell phone so that I could answer, "Hi, this is Liz Funk . . ." like in all the movies where the heroines work at magazines.

Now I am at the point where I *have* to wear nice outfits and don't have the liberty to have the voicemail greeting on my cell phone as: *"Hello? . . . Hello? . . . Hello? . . . Oh, right, I'm not here. Haha, tool! . . . I bet you thought I was and just started talking to me like a real conversation. Leave a message and I'll get back to you, if I like you. Thus, if you don't hear from me, you'll know why!"* Now that I'm finally "growing up," I find myself wishing I could be young again. But, wait . . . I *am* young. So why do all my overachieving friends and I feel so old?

Because being overachieving is inherently aging.

There are some Supergirls turning back the clocks. Lily Allen, the highly acclaimed British pop singer and young feminist, told the World Entertainment News Network in June 2007 that she plans to retire at age 30, having worked so hard during her adolescence: "What I'm going to do is work really hard, trying to make as much money as I can, then retire when I'm 30 and have my childhood. I'll just sit in the countryside, ride quad bikes all day, and have my own paintball course." Celebrities like Tara Reid, Paris Hilton, and Britney Spears were thrust into the public sphere during their late teens and worked tirelessly, shouldered endless criticism, and experienced pressure far exceeding what's appropriate for their ages. Subsequently, now that all three notorious starlets are in their mid- to late 20s, they have begun to act like adolescents, drinking recklessly, wearing miniskirts without underwear and sheer shirts while braless, and ignoring the explicit requirements made of them.

This has a *major* trickle-down effect: no offense to some of my slightly older readers, but I think today's 20-somethings are a little less mature than their predecessors. I think it really has to do with this concept of wanting to exist in "Neverland" to make up for lost time from having to focus on the War of 1812 and SATs and stupid student debt while only 16 years old.

I'm doing my best to enjoy what's left of my youth. But it's not appropriate for Supergirls who had their childhood and adolescence abruptly encroached upon to try to live in Neverland and make up for lost time by acting childish. It's okay to be afraid of aging and getting old, because we Supergirls were kind of robbed when it came to enjoying adolescence. Instead, young women need to hold the institutions accountable that perhaps took away their childhood and adolescence ahead of schedule. They need to call out our sexist society on the expectations that it gives girls, teachers who give out too much homework, colleges that are too hard to get into (and the TV shows and magazines that promote them as the only options for successful students). After all, if today's Supergirls can't be young and irresponsible and frivolous again, then perhaps they can do their best to create a world for their own kids where it's okay to be young and irresponsible and frivolous.

Thus, the issue of being young and free versus assiduous and work obsessed becomes really intensified going from high school to college. College presents its own internal contradictions of encouraging students to enrich themselves and mature while putting a very high premium on partying and socializing. It's another round in the game of doing it all and trying to make it look effortless . . . only this time, Supergirls have to take on this charade while a little intoxicated. Can they keep up the act?

Or, is college, with its expectation that young people let loose, party, and try their hand at keg stands, a good time for young women to try out relaxation and moderation? After all, college is when young people should develop the habits that they'll carry into their adulthood. So, will Supergirls try to keep up the "perfect" charade or will they find themselves? Or, better yet, can collegiate Supergirls have their beer and drink it, too?

chapter three

"I'm Really Not *That* Smart"

Supergirls Succeed in College and Beyond . . .
by Working (and Playing) Twice as Hard
as Anyone Else

....

To those of you who received honors,
awards and distinctions, I say well done.
And to the C students, I say you too may
one day be president of the United States.
—George W. Bush, in his commencement address
at Yale University, May 2001

It's a myth that all the girls who are hyperorganized and high
strung in high school go crazy during college, drinking forties
on the street corners and getting random body parts pierced.
But it's not entirely untrue. Supergirls have a wide spectrum of
experiences in college. Some young women juggle everything
they did in high school, plus an internship, a research project
they earned from helping a professor, a "college marriage," and
their newfound freedom. But some Supergirls have breakdowns,

some Supergirls go *wild,* some Supergirls really question themselves . . . and most Supergirls conceal all of their inner stress from the world.

Some Supergirls "recover" and learn a balance of work and play that will sustain them through college and into their first job. But, of course, that's not where the interesting—or realistic—stories are. What is also interesting is how college culture teaches girls what their roles are as women and prepares them for the years to come as Supergirls . . . and how some Supergirls think their every move in college will dictate how their lives will work out in their 20s.

Allie, Age 20, George Washington University

The George Washington University is so alive it practically has a pulse, and you can hear it beating the second you step on campus. Everyone on campus seems to be going places—literally and figuratively. The perfectly wardrobed students walk quickly, with their heads held high, pumping their arms, causing their designer messenger bags to bounce at their hips. The campus radiates a certain energy, probably due to the fact that the grads are likely to become senators, political journalists, or lawyers (and due to the coffee that students suck down like it's elixir from the fountain of youth). In the summer, Washington, D.C., is hot as hell, but virtually all of Washington is air-conditioned, so it's still pleasant; in the spring, the blooming cherry blossoms decorate the campus; in the winter, it's bleak and a little cold, but also regal and energized; and in the fall, students are too busy to notice the weather.

Allie is *the* GW student. She is in a classroom in a high-rise GW building, dressed fashionably in chic rain boots, pinstriped gauchos, and a satin pink tunic before the average college student has haphazardly swung his or her arm at the alarm clock's "snooze" button. Although she was born and bred in the slow-talking south (Atlanta, *Jo-Ja* is home for her), she certainly isn't slow-moving. Allie's 8am class is about Women in Sports and Title IX. Her medium-length light brown hair has been straightened, she is in full makeup, and she doesn't even look tired. And I reiterate: it's 8am! I consider myself an overachiever, but my 9 or 10am wakeup is nonnegotiable, even during the school year (although this comes with the understanding that a 1am bedtime for me is a luxury).

"I try to schedule my classes so they can fulfill requirements and make my schedule accommodating of work and internships. It doesn't really matter to me whether my classes are that interesting—some of mine aren't—so I happened to be really lucky that my 8am class is really fun," she says. Allie sits up straight taking notes throughout the class, even as the professor turns on a movie, which in the college student world is a cue to doze off.

After class, Allie and I swing by one of the campus's three Starbucks, all of which accept the school meal plan as payment, which is mobbed with pretty girls with their skinny jeans tucked into their knee-high leather boots, graduate students in expensive sweaters and nice skirts, and the errant guy in a sweatshirt and jeans. The students stand in a winding line, order triple-shot grande caramel macchiatos and venti coffees so big you can bathe in them if you don't finish them. This might imply that the students here are a little bit too wired . . . but they look composed and flawless, laughing with one another, revealing freakishly white teeth.

"The female students here seem to feel as though they have to compensate for their power," says Dr. Bonnie Morris, a professor of women's studies at George Washington University. "It's as though they feel they have to be charming and sweet to make up for being ambitious. They all want perfect résumés, but they really exert themselves to seem playful and carefree."

Allie fits in with this scenario. After her morning class, she grabs a coffee and runs to her first job of the day, at University Events, where she helps plan events and activities on campus that often involve famous people and always involve a lot of mental endurance. It would be inaccurate to say that Thursday is Allie's "long day," because so is Wednesday and Friday . . . and Monday and Tuesday, too. In fact, on Monday, Allie has an 8am class before an entire day of interning at the Girl Scouts D.C. office, and on Friday, she works half of the day at her on-campus job and half of the day at Girl Scouts . . . while balancing sixteen credit hours.

"The thing is," she explains to me, "I know that I want to be a lobbyist. And I know how to get from A to B, and essentially, every move I make will affect how quickly I get to that goal and to what extent I fulfill it. Like, every little thing you do right now will affect this plan."

Whoa.

Allie is well on her way to fulfilling this plan. She spent the past summer interning full-time for a political nonprofit dedicated to helping pro-choice Democrat women get into office, and she is an absolute firecracker at her internship. The next day at her internship, she sits at her desk for almost five hours working on a project with her officemate, a GW graduate student and fellow intern. Allie doesn't even take a coffee break during the entire afternoon. In fact, she stares intently at her computer screen, stopping only to smooth out her skinny jeans and cable knit sweater. And with her sixth-floor office view of Washington offering a distant gaze at the brownstones below and the leather upholstery decorating the office, the internship totally beats classes.

"The thing about being in school," says Megan, Allie's

officemate, a friendly redhead in her late 20s, "is that you have to make sure you appreciate it. Like, I took time off between doing my undergrad at University of California–Santa Cruz and coming to GW because I knew that I needed some time in the real world to figure out how badly I wanted more education."

Last year, Allie and her current roommate, a fast-talking, pretty Supergirl from Indiana, and four other girls—all Supergirls—lived in a university-owned brownstone together in hip Foggy Bottom. "On days when we were all stressed out and panicking, someone would be like, 'Who wants to take one for the team and off herself so the rest of us can get A's?'"

Some students don't take this pressure to heart, namely, the guys. "We joke that the guys here are either total slobs or gay," says Allie. "But the ideal of the 'average' GW girl is definitely hard to achieve," Allie tells me, double-crossing her legs and taking a bite of a chicken pesto sandwich at lunch. "She wears denim miniskirts over black leggings, UGG boots, a really wide headband, and she's Jewish," she says. Allie thinks that the standards for what it means to be female apply to all the social groups in the student body: "There's just this image in going to GW that I think a lot of the girls here want to keep up with."

Obviously, Allie keeps up with—if not sets the pace for—this race for accomplishments and an appeal of effortless perfection. In fact, on Thursday, she doesn't seem to sit still and relax until 8pm when *The Office* comes on . . . and even then, she is painting her nails and entertaining her friend John who comes over—who she insists is "just a friend"—but she still has to laugh at his jokes. "Sometimes I'll go out on Thursdays because some of the bars here have 18+ nights, so you can get wasted with your friends beforehand and then show up, but it gets a little exhausting." Although, if she was tired, Allie would never seem to indicate it, because every night when we would say good-bye for the evening, she still seemed like she could go on working for another few hours . . . and on some occasions, she worked well into the night after I left and still looked good the following morning.

Leah, Age 18, State University of New York at Albany

Leah has style. The 18-year-old is a freshman at the University at Albany, one of the four universities in New York State's SUNY public college system, known for its big parties, prime location, and strong science research programs. I met Leah when she contacted me after reading an opinion article I had penned for Long Island's daily newspaper *Newsday* about the criminal cost of private college; Leah told me that although she had her pick of colleges with her 4.0 GPA and exhaustive list of extracurriculars, she chose UAlbany largely because of the full scholarship they offered her, which would alleviate financial constraints on her family.

Sipping a gingerbread latte in a Starbucks in a tony shopping plaza in Albany, she's wearing jeans, a headband, and a Burberry scarf tied and tucked into her North Face. In fact, this is more or less her uniform for the next few days—nice jeans, designer scarf, and a North Face—although she switches up her handbags, alternating between a Coach purse and a Vera Bradley tote. She has curly brownish red hair that she either puts in a ponytail or pushes back with a headband. She has a spirited laugh and is always smiling, which could be a part of why she has so many friends.

Leah seems to be having the quintessential college experience: the kind of college experience that you would expect to see in a teen lit book, a CW TV series, or a movie about the ideal college life. She lives in the freshman quad, where four long buildings are arranged in a square around the twenty-two-floor tower where students live in suites with six students for the three bedrooms, a bathroom, and a little center hallway. Leah lives with five other girls who are from everywhere from Westchester to Texas, on a floor where it always seems dark and smells like perfume. The hallways are papered with seductive ads from magazines, but "I don't think they mean anything. I think the RA just pasted them there to be decorative," Leah says. The campus is papered in flyers for upcoming club meetings, political events, and even parties. On the weekends, Leah and her friends go to the crew team house to hang out and drink, or to the "student ghetto" of downtown Albany, where freshmen are encouraged to come to house parties and pay $5 for a big red cup with unlimited refills at the keg. This frivolity aside, however, Leah's days are scheduled down to the minute—she runs from clubs to class to meetings to work. Virtually every minute of her day between 10am and 10pm is accounted for in some kind of activity.

At lunch, we sit with two of her friends from the crew team, one of Albany's more elite teams, given the flagging interest among the campus in the football team. Both of Leah's friends are big good-looking guys who have a surprising interest in my women's studies major; one of the guys, according to Leah, is quite the feminist. Both guys are enrolled in a class about the intersections of gender, race, and class in society; one comes from Seneca Falls and knows a remarkable amount about the history of women's rights, and the other is a bioethics major who plans to advocate for abortion rights and stem cell research. The latter guy asked me who my favorite feminist was and why I liked studying feminism . . . questions that I personally had never pondered. What I also hadn't pondered was that there were guys this open-minded and engaged at UAlbany, a state school that has a bit of a party rep.

"There is a big stereotype here about Albany . . . there are negative connotations," Leah explains to me, detailing the sorority sisters who seem to care only about getting into parties and being pretty, and the meathead guys. "But they're not the majority. It's just that they are present and they are, you know, what people expect at the school. But I think the majority of the kids here are people like those guys and me, who are smart and care about the world and have ambitious goals despite these stereotypes."

Sitting on Leah's windowsill is the 300-something-page yearbook that Leah made *by herself* during her senior year of high school. She clocked pretty much every Saturday and Sunday senior year working on the yearbook to produce a product that took an entire staff of kids and an advisor a calendar year to make at my high school. "We had a yearbook class," Leah explains, "but it got cut and we weren't going to have a yearbook, so I took it on myself to make it for my grade. We couldn't graduate without a yearbook." The final product is amazing . . . it's the kind of hard work that you might expect from a kid headed to Yale, and I wonder whether Leah feels bizarre about manufacturing a yearbook—complete with sports team pages and rosters, ads, messages from parents, and photos from dances—that probably could have made her a shoo-in for any school she liked. "Sometimes I do feel like I settled," Leah says. "I've thought about transferring once so far this semester. But I have such a great deal here and I'll be able to graduate without debt . . . so I try not to think too much about where else I could have gone."

College Life

The overachiever culture from high school appears to taper off in college, but it really only seems that way because it takes a different form. Unlike high school, people's ambition is more private. Whereas you know who is taking however many AP classes and which sports they play on and how late practice goes until, college overachieving is more mysterious: no one knows how many credit hours their friends are taking, what clubs they're in, and what internships they're doing . . . unless they ask.

"I was crazy in high school," says Kayla C., a 2007 Wellesley College graduate who works in politics. "I had swim practice every day, did tons of clubs, did extra projects in class because *I wanted to*. I was at school really between 7 in the morning and 8 at night running between classes and clubs and sports practice, and then I came home and showered and did homework and only got a few hours of sleep every night. It was really insane. But in college, that kind of do-every-club, take-every-hard-class-possible mentality wasn't really present."

For Cynthia, now a sophomore at the University of Arizona, her freshman year at college was about disproving the stereotypes about what happens when tigers (and teenage girls) are released from their cages. "My mom doesn't know how to read and write, and in this world that's a very powerful tool. At eight I was writing checks, and at ten I was reading bills for her. For me, it was *I don't want to do this, I want to be selfish*—in a good way. I had to raise my three little sisters with her . . . and no girl should have to deal with that pressure. Then it was just work, work, work, and no play. I didn't have a childhood. I was such a ball of stress in high school, I barely even laughed."

When Cynthia left for Tucson to attend the University of Arizona, she had a rebirth. "It was like, 'This is my first taste of freedom.' People have always said, *Cynthia is going to go to college and go crazy*. But for once I'm having this balance." To put it bluntly, it sounds like Cynthia is living for the first time. "I have a good head on my shoulders. I've made some stupid mistakes. My mom doesn't know, and I took care of it on my own. Part of the problem was that I wasn't allowed to date and stuff when I lived with my parents. You want to learn in the little ball field about your sexuality and your body and who you are . . . but at college, I just got thrown in with the big sharks." However, it sounds like Cynthia is doing okay: she's just as cognizant as ever that grades are important and that her GPA is key to getting into law school . . . but she is also well aware of the fact that a B isn't the end of the world.

But this isn't to say that many students don't continue the behaviors they adopted in high school. "On the first day of class, I would already have my books, and by the first weekend, I would do as much homework as I could for the semester; I would read the books that would be assigned in November. I felt like I had to be one step ahead because I thought I'd be overwhelmed doing the work at the regular pace . . . although, of course I wouldn't be, because I was already doing it five times as fast as you were supposed to," says Kayla R., a recent graduate of George Washington University who plans to enroll in Harvard Graduate School next year. "There was also this issue that the women on campus were supposed to look a certain way and act very sure of themselves and be able to accomplish anything at the drop of a dime. . . . These were behaviors that seemed a little more sophisticated than high school overachieving."

Not to mention, there is no age discrimination when it comes to Supergirls. Christy, a midwestern Supergirl, attended college in Kansas and it wasn't for her, so she honed her talents and drive, and spent time working for Getty Images and Microsoft. An avid photographer, she started her own photography business and has been living in Seattle for the past eight years. Only recently did she decide to return to school and study at the

University of Washington, pursuing a women's studies major. "Right now I'm holding a 3.9 GPA. . . . I really just threw myself into school as a way to heal and because I'm so passionate about what I'm learning. I hope what I learn in school will help me to learn to end violence against women. I was thrilled when I got A's in each class. When I saw that, I was like, 'How did I pull that off with all the other stuff going on in my life?'"

Obviously, the pressure to be perfect on college campuses takes a different form. In high school, Supergirls want to be the girl next door and garner head pats and appreciation from school administrators, friends' parents, and peers. In college—especially given the anonymity of many sprawling college campuses—the pressure on Supergirls seems more about being someone's hot girlfriend, being sleek and elegant and charming, and practicing how to live an adult life. Although many people still picture college as a time of skipping class, eating pizza for breakfast, and waking up next to some guy and saying, "What's your name again?"—surely a product of the media—such a carefree existence is hard to imagine for a Supergirl. And while Supergirls know they're not alone in their stresses, the pressure to keep up and succeed can be alienating. So when I reached out to department chairs and professors at several different colleges, asking them to post my request for interview subjects on their student Listservs, my inbox was inundated within hours with e-mails from young women talking about the silent pressure

> "My friends are generally over-achievers, or at least my college friends are. My friend Allee once lived in the arts building for a couple weeks in order to perfect her ceramics for her upcoming art show. . . . And all this stress is expected not to affect our classwork. I'm not sure how that works."
>
> **—Patricia, age 20**

and expectations weighing them down and totally frizzing them out.

At Syracuse University, Agatha, a junior in the school's famed S.I. Newhouse School of Communications, sees a lot of students running around trying to achieve in order to have a great college experience marked by popularity and recognition, but also to live up to the school's reputation and earn kudos from alumni who might help get them jobs. "Kids take really hard classes and get involved in a lot of clubs to try and network as much as they can, and it's partly to make friends, but it's also an indication of the pressure here to try and live up to the Syracuse name."

What's also interesting, and probably a great problem at Syracuse (given the school's hard-partying reputation), is balancing work with partying, both part of the Supergirl requirement, given how social status is just as important as grades. Says Kayla R., the GW Supergirl: "It was a little bit of a struggle sometimes. There were nights when I'd go out and have a good time but decide to stop drinking early and leave a little before last call so the next day or the rest of the weekend could be productive. I'd definitely be thinking about it."

"I loved my undergrad experience," says Jessica, who attended the University of Central Arkansas. "I went to parties, I went on spring break adventures to Florida and the Gulf Coast, but I still got to be kind of that academic person. I was on color guard for the marching band, I was on the residence hall council, and I worked on the school newspaper." Jessica loved what she was doing . . . but she took on a little too much, and it started to show. "I never had body image issues in college, but I was losing weight quickly. I remember my mom coming to one of the games at school and she said to me, 'You look really thin.' My body suffered in trying to do so much—I didn't sleep enough, I didn't eat enough. It was hard to find the balance for myself without my family around. I think a lot of undergrads fall into that trap of trying to have fun—maybe too much fun—and also trying to be successful."

Personally, during my first year at college away from home, Thursdays were for partying moderately, whether it was a happy hour drowned in margaritas with friends from the school newspaper or a bottle of wine with girlfriends in front of *Grey's Anatomy*. Friday was the night to go totally all out in SoHo or Greenwich Village with a pack of my friends, with Saturday morning cleared out for recovery and downtime, and Saturday evenings and all day Sunday were for getting down to work.

"I think college has definitely been a struggle of wanting to achieve academically and take advantage of as many opportunities as possible, but also have a really good time and get to know a lot of people and have that stereotypical college experience," says Marie, both a notorious overachiever and social butterfly at my school, Pace University. "But then again, because I didn't get into Yale, now I'm a little bit like, *Screw it. I wasted high school studying to try to achieve something that clearly wasn't possible, and I'm not going to do that again for college.* I'm having fun now. . . . You can't do everything you want to do to the extreme that you want to do it in college: it's impossible."

Marie's best friend, Cara, another serious Supergirl, chimed in at this point in our conversation: "Plus, I think there is this feeling that one can just skate through college, partying at night and going to class hung over and doing homework and projects at

> "I didn't get into Yale. Now I'm a little bit like, *Screw it. I wasted high school studying to try to achieve something that clearly wasn't possible, and I'm not going to do that again for college."*
> —**Marie, age 19**

the last minute, but I don't think that's really true. Things like that take real effort."

Dr. SuEllen Hampkins, who served as the psychologist for Smith College, saw intense stress among the Supergirl-heavy campus and a lot of pressure. The students she counsels "talk about their sense of what they need to do to have a successful life, pressures from parents, and feeling like if they weren't able to keep up the levels of high grades and achieve a perfect body, then they wouldn't be successful or they wouldn't be happy. . . . It's complicated for the college because we want to promote academic excellence, but at the same time we want to promote the health of the students."

Many college administrations don't seem to be particularly nervous about their overachieving students. As Allie noted, there are three different Starbucks on the GW campus that accept the meal plan as payment; at many colleges, coffee is sold in every dorm, academic building, and cafeteria, and Red Bull or similar energy drinks are generally available in these locations as well. Most colleges will allow students to take eighteen or nineteen credits as part of their full-time matriculated tuition, which at many schools means tons and tons of homework; students can take more credits if they get an academic advisor's approval and pay extra per credit.

Although college professors are generally known for commitment to the education of young people and tweed ensembles, sometimes they aren't the most understanding about student stress. Says Joanna, a student at Russell Sage College, a women's college in Troy, New York: "I feel it has become sort of expected that you are a stressed-out basket case in college; otherwise you aren't doing enough—at least among myself and those who I know are the high achievers. I even know professors who have had said to a student who was asking for an extension on a paper,

'How much did you sleep last night?' and after the student told her six hours, the professor said, 'Well, that's more sleep than I get,' and refused the extension."

Dominique, a recent graduate of the University of Chicago, had always been impressive: she lived in Paris as a child and not only caught up with the French elementary school curriculum, which is "much more advanced," but also learned French in the process (now she's also fluent in Polish and very proficient in Italian and Latin). When she enrolled in high school back in the United States, she was underchallenged and began taking courses at the University of Kansas. "It would get a little crazy sometimes, with my mom shuttling me from clubs after school to classes at the college and then back home for dinner and then back to school, but I really enjoyed it."

Dominique was enrolled in a host of AP classes and honors curriculums at her high school, but she still felt fairly unburdened by all the tasks on her plate. By the time she was graduating from high school, she was just shy of completing a bachelor's degree at the University of Kansas. "I didn't go on and do that last course and stop college there, however, because I wanted to be a normal kid and have that traditional college experience." So Dominique enrolled that fall at the University of Chicago. "It was *a lot* of work: people joke that it's like 'The University of Chicago: Where Fun Goes to Die.'" However, Dominique did exceedingly well in school and still had time to participate in clubs and student government, as well as travel. She graduated with a double major and high honors, and was accepted into Yale's graduate programs, to dually pursue a graduate degree in engineering and a M.D. in neurophysiology. "I'm really excited!" she beamed.

Although the graffiti in a stall of one of the women's bathrooms at Yale reads, "The pressure here could make me kill myself," contrary to popular stereotypes, it's not just big-name schools that serve up big pressure. Joanna defines Russell Sage, her college of four hundred–something students, as high pressure, and says Cassandra, a recent graduate from a small liberal arts college on the west coast, "The students were academic masochists. It was like everyone there loved a good ass kicking. Because of the school's liberal reputation, I don't think people thought us to be so overachieving . . . but I ended up getting into twenty of the best sociology graduate programs because of it. . . . Some kids developed real emotional problems from the stress."

But Didn't Elle Woods Go to Harvard Law?

College is very much a media-fed experience. News tickers are prominently portrayed on many college campuses, wifi Internet is everywhere from the library to the dorms to the grassy quad (which, in the best of purposes, helps students check their e-mail for class information and projects [and Facebook!], and for the worst of purposes, enables students to check the snarky gossip blog PerezHilton.com at several intervals a day), and actually, Facebook in itself is a major outlet of DIY media that puts pressure on young women to portray their lives a certain way. So, naturally, the media has tons of ties to the lives of Supergirls in college.

There are lots of celebrity Supergirls who went to good colleges: Claire Danes went to Yale, Julia Stiles to Columbia, and Lauren Bush to Princeton; believe it or not, Jessica Simpson considered applying to Harvard, and Hilary Duff took an online class with the Ivy League favorite. Angelina Jolie goes to Africa and helps refugees; Hilary Duff has worked with more charities than she has pairs of shoes. Christy Carlson Romano played a diehard, exhausted Supergirl on the Disney Channel show *Even Stevens,* while the Olsen twins delivered the overworked Supergirl persona in at least two straight-to-video films aimed toward young girls. Kelly Clarkson, one of the most ambitious young singers in the United States, told *ELLE* magazine in spring 2007, "For most of my childhood I was walking on eggshells trying to make everyone happy."

Reese Witherspoon played probably the scariest Supergirl in the 1999 movie *Election,* and the most attractive—and most perplexing—Supergirl in the 2002 movie *Legally Blonde.* On that note, the media's portrayal of women as flakes or stupid girls has endlessly complicated the way that the media cultivates Supergirls. The negative portrayal of women in the media as sexual objects and as secondary to men has fueled a culture where young women are raised to feel less powerful than they actually are and Supergirls' accomplishments are lesser than they are. Deep down inside, all Supergirls (including Elle Woods) know that getting into Harvard Law is, in fact, incredibly difficult.

The presence of high-achieving women and Supergirls as real and fictional characters in the media does not mean that the media is a friend to young women. In fact, the media's portrayal of young women as stupid sex objects could be at the root of why there is so much confusion for young women in college about their appropriate roles: whether it's okay to be smart (or whether being smart needs to be compensated for by getting excessively drunk at frat parties to be cute), and how to balance work and school with being popular and fun.

The rise of ditzy girls in the media has *completely* garbled the role of what it means to be a young woman. Even more so when the most famous ditzy young women—like Paris Hilton, Jessica Simpson, and Britney Spears—are some of the richest, most successful young women in the entertainment industry, the beauty industry, and the fashion industry.

In doing research for her book, *Math Doesn't Suck: How to Survive Middle School Math Without Breaking a Nail,* Danica McKellar heard from girls who admitted that they were "dumbing themselves down" to get boys to like them. "When we have people like Jessica Simpson confusing chicken and tuna, it's clearly a calculated move to get attention, because she knows people will say, 'Oh, how cute!' But that's a pretty damaging example for young women to follow."

In 2005, when Victoria Beckham confessed to *Chic,* a Spanish magazine, that she had never read a book in her life, what kinds of messages did she send out? That being lusted over and accepted is not something that requires brains? It's these messages that make life so confusing for Supergirls: When our teachers and professors are telling us to be smart and savvy and successful, but the magazines in the library or in the employee break room divulge how great it is to be dumb and imply that women aren't supposed to be brilliant, what are we supposed to do? How can we Supergirls have a shot at Harvard when Posh Spice, arguably a total embodiment of the female ideal today, is arguably also one of the least literary people on the planet?

As such, no offense to Posh Spice, but another conflict that creates a lot of confusion for young women is this: the majority of the women who are idolized in the media, who represent what a woman should be, contribute *absolutely nothing* to society. How are Supergirls supposed to change the world when Paris Hilton and Lindsay Lohan are the closest we have to mainstream-accepted spokeswomen for our generation?

What young women have to keep in mind is that media—whether it's TV, music, books, movies, or the ads that come with them—is not created solely to entertain, and many of the people creating it haven't considered (and may not even care) what kind of effect it will have on viewers. Says Dr. SuEllen Hampkins, a psychologist who focuses on women's issues, "It's hard for people to understand that Madison Avenue does not have the well-being of young women in mind. The media isn't meant to enhance people's lives or change the world . . . it's there to make money. The media is a *business*."

"There is much less media literacy among young people in America today," says Marisa Meltzer, a magazine freelance writer. "America is one of the only countries that doesn't teach media literacy in school, so young women see something on television and directly translate that image into their lives."

It's okay to worship celebrity Supergirls like Anne Hathaway, to screen *Legally Blonde* once every six months, and, *ulch*, to whip out old *Newlyweds* DVDs when you're spending a Saturday morning in bed recovering from a crazy night at the lacrosse house. However, Supergirls have to keep in mind that they don't have to be as multitalented as Anne Hathaway, that getting into Harvard Law is actually incredibly hard, that girls who are successful don't have to ascribe their success to mere happenstance, and that women who will actually go to Harvard (and college at all!) don't pretend not to know the difference between chicken and fish.

Stay Smart, But Be Sexy, Too

Koren Zailckas wrote in *Smashed: Story of a Drunken Girlhood*: "College, like most life experiences, doesn't look as good as it does on TV. Specifically, it doesn't look as good as it does on MTV. The network's coverage of spring break first premiered when I was five, from which time I honestly believed that college was what I saw in their ninety-second promo spots. . . . I imagine other people still do think this."

As said, the media creates lots of stereotypes about over-achiever colleges: that the fraternities and sororities dominate campus, that kids Facebook through class, and that students have pizza for breakfast and Adderall for a midnight snack. Every campus creates its own culture, and at each school, the roles for what it means to be a good girl can change just as drastically . . . although working relentlessly is a constant.

When Erin, a tireless Supergirl and women's rights activist, was growing up in Las Vegas, the inconsistent roles for women she observed were quite baffling for her: between the showgirls and the rich wives, the expectations for what she was supposed to become definitely got confusing. "I mean, it's *Las Vegas*—the available roles for women really aren't that positive. This one time, I was on a field trip and I told one of the moms chaperoning the trip that I liked her coat. She told me, 'Well one day, maybe you'll have a husband who will buy one for you.' But when I got to the University of Chicago, the expectations on young women were really different. Of course, there was still sexism, but being smart and self-sufficient were really important, too. Being a professional, powerful woman was understood as what the female students were to do."

"I'm originally from West Virginia, so coming here was a huge culture shock for me," says Kelly, a kind and very bubbly girl in her final year at Southern Methodist University. "There is just such a different role for women on this campus. People put a lot more effort in their looks—they're a lot more fashionable, but I think it's part of this larger goal for the girls to look perfect and be pretty every day. . . . It's sort of expected that the girls are supposed to wear dresses everywhere, with their hair blown dry and their makeup done nicely. I had to go out and buy a ton of sundresses when I got here . . . it's very old-fashioned."

Patricia, another SMU student, feels really dissatisfied by the limiting female ideal at SMU: "[The typical SMU girl] is the sorority sister who was a popular cheerleader in high school and whose daddy bought her an expensive car as a graduation present. I honestly can't tell most of them apart. I guess she faces the pressure to look pretty and expensive. . . . They can't drive and have nearly killed me twice in their shining, expensive cars. . . . Then they grow up to become expensive trophy wives and continue to drive badly."

Within the context of a conservative Baptist college, Kelly also doesn't think the way these women act is just for show: "My friends and I joke about how the girls who are trying to look perfect and act as though they have it all together are coming here to get their MRS . . . but a lot of the time, we're not actually joking. . . . I think the broader campus feeling is that many women come here to work really hard, become 'known,' and then find a husband and settle down. . . . There is a big although kind of subtle push for the women to be subordinate, like always wearing dresses and always looking and acting as though they want to please. In fact, I think some of the sororities here actually tell the sisters they have to go to the football games to support the guys and that they have to wear dresses."

Similarly, in the wake of the lacrosse scandal at Duke University in 2006, when three players were accused of raping a stripper hired to perform at one of their parties (although charges were never brought), *Rolling Stone* published an investigative article that focused on how young women on campus were expected to act in a supporting role to the guys and indicated the presence of Supergirls long before the word existed.

The article quoted Donna Liskert, director of Duke University's Women's Center, who said that female undergraduates feel tremendous pressure "to excel both academically—get the right grades, the right internships, move your life in the right path—but then you also need to excel physically, if you will," with perfect hair, skin, clothes, makeup and a size-four body. . . .

"Our undergraduate women at Duke are the best of the best," she says. "They're so smart, so driven, top of their class, student-government presidents, lettered in every sport." But when it comes to their personal lives, men set the social rules. "They throw the parties, they create the expectations, they create the standards, and these women—these incredibly smart women—on some level, being accepted by their peers is so important that they put aside their own values and standards. They dumb it down."

This article is brilliant for several reasons. It boldly notes that the "mainstream" female students at Duke, who went to fraternity parties and danced on tables in bikinis and miniskirts, saw their fitting role as women during the Duke rape scandal not to join in the anti-rape activism but to start campaigns in defense of the Duke lacrosse players; this role, supporting guys who hired strippers at a campus that draws some of the smartest (or best-connected) students in the country, was the one most appropriate for them. Similarly, Reitman discusses how sisters in top sororities were "honored" by invitations to fraternity hazing events where they pour chocolate sauce on one another and the pledges have to lick it off and were also honored by invitations to go to the boys' parties and serve them shots and cigarettes while dressed as Playboy bunnies.

Sorority sisters seem to be simultaneously loved and loathed by their female counterparts for one specific reason: many sorority houses widely broadcast images of themselves as effortlessly perfect.

"You can literally pick an SDT—Sigma Delta Tau—girl out of the crowd," a Syracuse student told me. "They all have long brown straight hair and really tan skin, and they walk around in denim miniskirts in the dead of winter." And Syracuse, with its freezing winters, gets pretty slushy. How do the sorority sisters take that? "I can't say that their effect on the student body here and on the roles for students is particularly positive."

"Wherever you go, there is an ideal for women—she has to be pretty, she has to be thin, and she has to not be assertive," says Cynthia, a sophomore at the University of Arizona. "I have the looks to be in a sorority, but I don't have the submissiveness."

Says Sasha, a UC–Berkeley sociology major: "There are thirty thousand people on this campus, about half of them women, who are all intelligent and socially aware and unique . . . but the four hundred sorority sisters who are pretty white girls with the huge sunglasses, expensive white sundresses, and long blonde hair, with their letters are the paradigm of what all the other women are supposed to look like and they represent all the other women. . . . There's this concept that all women, especially sorority women, need to follow this model of being the blonde, drunk Tri-Delt girl. . . . I think a lot of women are depressed because there is no space to explore what it's like to be a woman and explore alternate roles and illustrations of femininity." With this in mind, Sasha is a sorority sister, but Justine, Sasha's "big sister" in her sorority, thinks that their house tries to deconstruct some of the pressures. "Of course, we face the same pressure of all the other sorority sisters to be pretty and composed and, of course, smart, but we also try to have a lot of conversations about the expectations on us and why we're expected to look and act a certain way," says Justine. "In fact, we've tried to have group discussions with the whole sorority about the social demands made of us and whether we fulfill them, and we try to brainstorm how we can do what's right for us but still feel comfortable in our social cultures."

Sometimes, however, the sexism is a little more formal, a little more institutional: because Intisar, now a Midwest-based Supergirl, attended the ultra prestigious boarding school Phillips Exeter Academy, she was totally prepared for college. "[Boarding school] was a very collegial atmosphere: It was friendly, supportive. People were interested in hearing what you thought and really helped hone your interests. It was the most challenging and vibrant education system I've ever been in. I think I hit my intellectual peak when I was 18, and it's only gone downhill since."

Unfortunately, college life for Intisar paled by comparison. She headed off to college in Minnesota to study computer science, because she knew it was an increasingly important and pertinent field. The department wasn't very progressive: "I enjoyed working with computers, but there was so much sexism in the computer science department! I had teachers stand up in front of class and say, 'Women can't use this technology.' There was also a lot of racism and religious discrimination, but that was something I was used to. Honestly, my school was an old boys' club and an archaic department. There were some professors who were good, but . . . in one of my classes, in the first class it was half men, half women, and by the second class it was three-quarters men, and by the third class it was all guys except for myself and one other girl, because it was just such a hostile environment for women." Because feeling welcome in her studies and socially comfortable was a big priority for Intisar (as it should be!), she decided not only to leave the computer science department but to transfer. So, she ended up transferring to the University of Colorado at Boulder, a huge public school known for its huge parties and huge academics. Lucky for Intisar, she found a true place for herself: "I ended up graduating as an outstanding business student. It was such a better place for me."

On the contrary, at urban schools, there seems to be a double bind: the ideal female is one who makes the most of what the city has to offer, interning and studying while carving out some time for the smorgasbord of partying options the city has to offer (no offense to Boulder, but I don't think the University of Colorado is on the same playing field as New York to count as an "urban" school). Despite the temptation of Greenwich Village's twenty-four-hour tattoo parlors, countless drug dealers, and bohemian bars that serve virtually anyone over age 15, Diana, an NYU senior who attended a strict religious boarding school in Pennsylvania for high school, stayed a Supergirl. "The teachers freshman year expected so much of us, it's not even funny. They would say, 'You know, for students who were admitted to a Tier I school, your papers were very disappointing.'" Having been students who were raised to please people, Diana said her peers, especially her female peers, took their schoolwork to the next level.

"So I started taking Adderall to stay awake to study. It's really amazing stuff. Like, you take one pill, and all of the sudden, you have focus." Over the course of the next few years, Diana used the drug more and more until she overdosed and starting seizing from taking too much. After a period of serious self-reflection, Diana worked out her anxiety and no longer uses the drug, although she maintains, "It's really okay if you take it in moderation."

Diana has endured panic attacks, all-nighters, and immeasurable pressure. She's got it together now: over the years, she says, she learned how to balance working and having a life, and has the social circle to prove it. And on some level, her Supergirl approach to life has paid off: she has accepted a job offer for the fall with a healthy starting salary, she has a nice apartment, and her ambitious boyfriend is moving in with her over the summer.

Diana is successful and smart, but she definitely paid a price for her Supergirl habits. But, similar to Duke, she doesn't think the NYU boys have anywhere near this pressure on them.

The college world as a whole promotes lots of double standards. There is still the "guys score, girls become sluts" issue that has plagued young women since high school. On many campuses where parties in dorm rooms are limited due to drinking crackdowns, fraternities become the sole source of parties, and they can define who gets in, what attendees drink, and what attendees must wear to get it. On many campuses, the sororities must have "house mothers" (adults who supervise the daily goings-on at the house), but the fraternities don't; also, many sororities have "closed kitchens," where the doors to the kitchens are locked at night to prevent girls from binge eating and purging (or perhaps just eating), while could you ever picture a fraternity where the guys weren't allowed to eat at night? I guess skinny sorority sisters make more money for the national organization?

And many of these double standards seem in place to do one thing: prevent young women from achieving actual power and make it clear that in order to be viewed seriously, young women have some compensating to do. Young women can't have college be a time of pizza for breakfast, insatiable beer drinking, and underachieving. If young women can never be as good as the guys, then they can go for the next best thing . . . being as perfect as females can get, by working *all the time.*

Unfortunately for the Supergirls already growing battle-weary, this isn't about to change anytime soon, given that they go straight from college to the 20-something scene. Quarter-life crisis? More like "second puberty," only this time, a gal doesn't even get bigger breasts out of it.

chapter four

"It's No Big Deal . . ."

Supergirls Succeed in the "Real" World and Make
It All Look Effortless . . . Even When It's Not

You got into Harvard Law?
What, like it's hard?
—Reese Witherspoon as Elle Woods
in the 2001 movie *Legally Blonde*

Getting a job means a lot of different things to young women:
for some, it's validation; for some, it's power; and for some, it's
an excuse to buy an expensive ID card holder to use to swipe
into a skyscraper office building in a major city. The high school
and college years often provide a lot of positive enforcement
like awards ceremonies and lovingly awarded honors degrees.
But when success and standing ovations don't immediate ensue
in a Supergirl's 20s, life can become endlessly frustrating. The
office also presents unusual struggles with respect to femininity: Given that feminine power doesn't seem to be appreciated
in the office, how should Supergirls balance their femininity

when it's clear that it's better to act like a man on the path to a corner office? Also, an unfair pay gap for women keeps many Supergirls tied down by their purse strings. However, the 20s can also present some really wonderful life changes, like having an apartment or a house to call your own, developing into an adult alongside your friends, and picking out wineglasses and throw pillows.

Yolanda, Age 27, New York City

Midtown Manhattan is one of the most exciting parts of New York City. Madison Avenue is alive at 11am with tall, thin women in white button-down shirts tucked into high-waisted black skirts and freshly shaven guys, many of whom look absurdly young in light blue button-down shirts and ties. Older guys in dark suits casually hold a BlackBerry in their free hand and look bored waiting for the pedestrian street light to indicate "go." Everyone walks fast. The streets are lined with skyscrapers, offices for internationally known companies, and hotels with rich-colored awnings hanging over golden doors staffed by bored-looking doormen in uniforms with brass buttons and silly hats.

Yolanda is waiting for me in the regal lobby of one of Manhattan's biggest and most prestigious banks. She strides toward me in a professional yet chic and still feminine black suit, and gives me a firm handshake. She has brown doe eyes, warm brown hair, and shockingly white teeth; she's gorgeous, but you can also tell that if you were on *The Apprentice* with her, you wouldn't even want to fight her for the alpha (fe)male spot. Her speech is terse, her e-mails are short and to the point, and her tone is serious. But it has paid off.

At age 27, Yolanda is an assistant vice president and

relationship manager for one of New York's best banks.[1] The majority of those who hold the same job as her and work on the same team are decades older.

However, Yolanda doesn't handle just any foreign accounts; she is the relationship manager for the high-profile accounts of individuals with a net worth over $35 million who are interested in private banking. She works on a team with several other individuals who handle these high-status accounts in Africa, Europe, and the Middle East. Although they are all of the same rank and seniority, she is by far the youngest person on her team; in fact, the closest person in age to her is 35.

During the course of a day, Yolanda will check in on her clients and survey what their needs are, relate requests to other branches of her bank, make dozens of phone calls and send faxes, and check her e-mail about a billion times. Naturally, it's a wired profession that, as Yolanda says, requires constant contact with others and a love of not necessarily numbers but just talking and communicating.

Banking, especially in Yolanda's company, is traditionally a male-dominated field. And Yolanda, who isn't exactly gentle but does emanate a certain femininity, has had some navigating to do. "There are so many roles that women have to play in the office. They need to be tough powerhouses if they want to get promotions and raises and deals, but they also need to be sweet and empathetic to gain acceptance among the other women in the office, but they can't be too sweet because they need to be seen as reliable by the men." Although there isn't the sexist concept from the 1950s that if women are in the office, they better look

---

1   One condition of being able to include such a wunderkind like Yolanda in this book is that her bank requested that I veil its identity, which I will comply with. However, I can vouch for the fact that her job has major street cred . . . you've definitely heard of her bank.

damn good, there is still a bit of a push to be pretty: "Everyone in my office is polished. They make sure their clothes are fashionable, that their hair and skin looks good, that they keep their figures in check. It's not like you have to be stunning, but this definitely is an image-oriented business." Clothes for Yolanda, however, mean more than just stepping into a knee-length A-line skirt and a more conservative pair of pumps: "It's interesting: the second I step into this black suit and these pointy shoes, I feel myself change. I sit up straighter and throw my shoulders back, and I get more powerful and a little more assertive."

But Yolanda is still incredibly feminine and well dressed. "I like your glasses," I tell her. They're Prada, and her bag and shoes are Gucci. "Do you like fashion?"

"I like picking out clothes and some of the designer stuff, but I'm not *that* into it" she says and shrugs. "A few nights ago I went to the new floor opening at Saks"—Saks Fifth Avenue, that is—"because my coworkers and I got invites. It was actually really cute; it was like a scavenger hunt or something where all the designers had a table in their department and you got your little pamphlet stamped by them when you went to their table, and obviously this was just a ploy so you would see the new layout of the store and Saks could have its potential 'high-influence' or whatever shoppers get a first look at their new things . . . but when you turned in your little Saks 'passport' stamped from all the designers, you got a little Kate Spade passport holder at the end, and, of course, free drinks and hors d'oeuvres." Yum . . .

Speaking of good food, the lunch buffet at our restaurant is amazing. Yolanda and I served ourselves salad and candied sweet potatoes, grilled chicken, and rolls from the nicely arranged buffet, and even though it's only 11:30, every suit above 14th Street seems to be pouring in the place. And while the food is pay-per-pound, the insanely attractive guys in dress shirts and nice shoes are all-you-can-drool.

"I'm actually not interested in this kind of preppy guy. I don't think they're that cute, and anyways, if they're in your company, they're totally off-limits. It wouldn't help your case to fall for a guy in your office."

Hence, the way women comport themselves in the office doesn't just have to do with their beauty and fashion choices. According to Yolanda, young women on the job need to be conscious of the fact that the behaviors that they are conditioned into that make them more female can kill their office mojo: "You need to be sure that the femininity you are putting across is appropriate for the office. You especially have to be really careful with apologizing. I did a lot of apologizing when I first started working, but I don't anymore, especially if it wasn't my fault . . . but even if it was my fault, I try not to apologize. In this kind of setting, you don't want to take the blame for something. It's seen as a sign of weakness if you take the fall for something, especially if you didn't actually do it. People don't take the blame for things and they try to dodge it left and right, and because women are constantly apologizing for everything—even for things that they didn't do—it hurts their reputation and the way that they are viewed so much in this kind of environment," she says, forking through her Caesar salad.

But the converse of these actions, she feels, is just as bad: "Oh my God, there is this one woman on my team who yells. She has no authority to yell . . . she has the same position as everyone else, but she is always yelling at people, even our boss. . . . I think a lot of women think that if you want to be powerful or show power, you need to be mean and yell, when really, that's not how it works at all."

In fact, it's the bosses who sometimes yell at you. "I grew up in a traditional family, so I was kind of used to being yelled at; my parents are really old-fashioned, and if I did something wrong, they would *yell*. So if something goes wrong and my boss yells at me, it's not a big deal. But the younger women in the office, these all-American girls who have been raised to be perfect and please everyone, really seem to crumble when someone yells at them."

But, like these all-American girls, Yolanda has had her work insecurities. "Not thinking about work all the time has taken some serious effort. . . . I had to really consciously separate work from my life. Because you could let it take you over."

While Yolanda has had her struggles to make it in her 20s, her life seems kind of fabulous. She has a great clique of friends, many of whom she's known since middle school, who go out to trendy bars and clubs in the West Village on the weekend; a boyfriend who, weirdly, works for the same company as her; and unlike her peers in the banking world who have to appropriate significant portions of their salaries to paying off student debt, Yolanda is in decent shape. Because she grew up in Canada, Yolanda was able to take advantage of Canada's socialized education system, meaning she was able to attend the prestigious McGill University for an incredibly low $2,000 a semester. And because she moved out young and lived on her own during college, she became independent very early. "When I was in college, my parents would give me some money to live on, but I mostly paid my own rent and paid for my own food and clothes and living expenses. When I ran out of money, I would call my dad and ask for more, and he'd say, 'No, this is your responsibility. Figure it out.'" While this situation obviously didn't lend itself to experiencing the craziness of dorm life and other alcohol-sodden college rituals, Yolanda subsequently had fewer struggles with adulthood and the quarter-life crisis when she graduated from college.

And while she'll have some struggles in the future, like

deciding when to get married, possibly moving for work, and when to have kids, it sounds like if you approach your 20s and the office with Yolanda's cool, pragmatic philosophy, not only do things turn out okay, but you also pick up some designer freebies along the way. Hey—if it means free Kate Spade stuff, I might even consider banking.

Or . . . maybe not.

Wanting to Be a Hotshot

I'd wanted to write a book for years. In fact, I've written several book proposals and even a novel, but what has always surprised me about the professional world is that success doesn't come easily. For every op-ed piece I've had published, there are at least ten that haven't been. For every article I've written that came out of pitching a story, there are at least twenty (yes, *twenty*) that have been rejected or ignored. It was a harsh awakening, realizing that success doesn't come easily in the work world. After all, my teachers in high school and my college professors always rewarded my urge to want to do more, do things earlier than I should, and speak out about how I feel . . . whereas in the professional sphere, well, I think I'm going to have gray hair before the *New Republic* ever publishes me.

As soon as the tossed caps hit the ground at college graduation, Supergirls who are not geared toward further education often almost immediately end up in the workforce. Which has its perks: a job often comes with having a swipe card to get in a fancy office building, business cards, an excuse to buy the $90 Editor pants at Express (as well as an entire cute work wardrobe, like velvet blazers and conservative dark jeans), and a sense of work paying off. Unfortunately, for many of the women I talked with, the honeymoon ends within a few months.

In high school and college, there are clear-cut plans to becoming a hotshot: participate in as many clubs and difficult classes as possible, get on a first-name basis with as many administrators as possible, and get involved with community activities that are often the subject of media attention. But in the office, things are different. To get ahead, there is lingo to learn, politics to be wary of, an unsaid dress code to tiptoe around, and lots and lots of coffee to make (which is intensely frustrating for overachievers whose degrees in finance or business administration and theses discussing the sexism of the mainstream media are being put to use fueling someone else's brain with legal stimulants). And while there can often be major perks to an office environment— like networking events with an open bar, company spending accounts, and an excuse to buy more shoes—there can also be some less than pleasant circumstances.

Given that Supergirls paid their dues in high school trying to get into college and paid their dues in college trying to graduate, most feel weird completing entry-level tasks when they wrote huge research papers and learned formulas and equations and computer code in college.

During her first year on the job, Emily, a graduate of the George Washington University, had a bit of trouble with office life. "The organization [I worked for] expected a lot of its employees, but it was difficult for me to not be the one putting the pressure on myself. It was odd, because I was part of a much larger team, and because the organization had been around for so long, it had lots of set ways of doing things. . . . It was very, very difficult. I was depressed for a lot of the year. . . . I think [my younger colleagues and I] struggled because we had come from a position on campus where we were really in strong leadership positions, then brought to an organization where we were not given the same creative room." Emily left after a year, but she views her first job as a growing experience: "I can't stress enough how much I learned about an international organization. It's just that the job that I have now is a better fit; I have much more creative direction."

While heading to a school with name-brand recognition like Harvard or Williams at least gives the reassurance that everything will be legit and that it will be at least a little challenging, this isn't necessarily true on the work front. One of my good friends recently got a full-time internship at a well-known fashion magazine, which she was so excited about, seeing it as a testament to her hard work in college. However, this kind of came crashing down on the first day of her internship when she was told by her boss, "Do not speak until spoken to." Given that all through high school and college, girls were rewarded for schmoozing and being impulsive, what are they supposed to do when they are given clear instructions to do nothing but organize boxes, fold clothes, and track shipments for forty hours a week? These are things that UPS and Gap employees are paid to do . . . so why should a Supergirl who has so adeptly displayed and honed her talents at brand-name schools have to do them?

Similarly, Laura Jeanne Hammond, the editor of the college admissions magazine *Next Step*, had a choice to make when she graduated from the University of Missouri, known for its excellent journalism program: she could head to New York and start at the bottom of a well-known magazine within a well-known company and work her way up to the top, or she could take a job at a smaller publication, which wasn't necessarily as well known but would allow her to do actual editing. "I think there is a real drive for young women to get the *right job* rather than be in the *right place*. I always had a dream of working at a magazine in

Washington, D.C., or in New York City, but I had to really look inside myself and decided what values I wanted to continue, whether I wanted the *right job* or if I wanted to do what was best for me. I had to weigh whether if I wrote two sentences for a top women's magazine would be better than doing more hands-on work at a smaller publication and I could live somewhere where all my family was, and have it be a better publication for me. A big magazine with little responsibility might have been perfect from a traditional life standpoint . . . but that wasn't what I wanted. I wanted to learn by doing." Naturally, she chose to work at *Next Step,* and within just a few years, Hammond became editor-in-chief and led the magazine to win several awards and distinctions!

When Intisar, a University of Colorado graduate, was faced with her job search, it took her a little while to do the requisite networking in Cincinnati to find a job in health care, specifically, consulting with hospitals for their

> "The organization [I worked for] expected a lot of its employees, but it was difficult for me to not be the one putting the pressure on myself."
>
> **—Emily, age 24**

business and supplies needs. It took her longer, however, to sort out what her priorities were for her job search. "I really had to think to myself, 'Do I want to help hospitals that have VIP services, which would be more glamorous kind of work, or do I want to work in the area where there is desperate need'? There are always people who want to be on this career path, but there are far fewer people who are well educated and well intentioned and have the privilege and luxury to work for serving people who have been failed by the system or a system that is being destroyed." After some serious soul searching, Intisar realized that she wanted to do the latter, working for hospitals with greater need. Did she take a pay cut? Probably. Is she more fulfilled in her work? Definitely.

Once Supergirls find a place that's a good fit for them, there is still some navigating to do, in terms of behaviors and personalities. To a certain extent, offices require a lot of Supergirl behavior. Attentiveness is a must, but the empathy and personal touch that most Supergirls have perfected is what get promotions. Helping others and taking on more tasks than necessary are almost always appreciated. While enforcing this damaging behavior isn't so hot, Supergirls' constant people-pleasing helps many ascend the corporate ladder (as long as it doesn't come off as annoying first!). Acting as though everything is great and under control and effortlessly perfect is what Supergirls do best . . . and also happens to be what makes bosses very, very happy.

Although, similar to how being a Supergirl and outdoing everyone else can cause some tension in high school and college social settings, doing 150 percent in the office isn't always such a hot idea either. "Being the new girl who works late every night and doesn't take a lunch and does lots of extra projects isn't always a good thing, not only from the burnout perspective, but in the sense of creating relationships with new coworkers," says Hannah Seligson, author of *New Girl on the Job: Advice from the Trenches.* "Working to that level of excess is not required, and it can really make your coworkers feel threatened by you and make them feel like you're there trying to outpace them and outdo them."

Other behaviors that young women have been conditioned into can hurt them. Although young women in our society are taught that talking in a high voice makes them sweet and cute, "I sometimes observe that when young women are in an office setting, their vocal placement is in a very high register. They sound tentative and insecure and as a result are not taken as seriously," says Cathy Wasserman, a Brooklyn-based life and executive career coach. "In contrast, if you hear someone speaking from a deeper place within themselves . . . you'll very likely see that their thoughts and opinions are listened to and seriously considered." Something that I notice among my friends who want to be writers or editors is that while we get a lot of validation for being young and cute, sometimes we play the "I'm young" card a little too much. Apparently this is kind of a universal problem. Says Hannah Seligson, "There are definite qualities associated with being young, but it's a very short-term strategy. . . . Young women need to do [a] professional persona, not phrase everything as a question, [and] write persuasively and assertively."

Plus, when girls are raised to "be nice" and accept blame, especially in the office where there are often confrontations and occasionally yelling, there is an automatic double bind for young women. "The concept of women being expected to be placating and to be peacemakers has deeps roots in Western society; it largely has to do with the role of women as nurturers . . . but it can be very damaging in modern society because this expectation that women are supposed to be nice prevents them from being able to bring up the problems and issues that they are experiencing," says Wasserman. "There is also a personal price to pay for placating in the office—inauthenticity."

It seems like guys have a lot less hurdles to navigate at work. The double standards in the office are overwhelming, and this people-pleasing and niceness is simultaneously the issue and at the core of the issue. "While it is more of an option than ever before for women to become leaders, the expectation is often that they should be 'nice leaders,'" says Wasserman. "Once again, their role is limited to one way of being and interacting that doesn't fit most women."

But that's not the only role that doesn't fit most women. . . .

New Problems with the Supergirl Role at Work

Jennifer Crisafulli, a fall 2004 contestant on *The Apprentice,* who herself was a hypercompetitive real estate mogul, told reporters that she enjoyed participating in fox hunting.

The other day, when I wanted to ask a guy I met at a bar for his phone number but expressed hesitation, my friend told me to "grow some balls."

> "My work is why I wake up in the morning . . . and something that I'm just really excited about. . . . I'm working for myself and working to advance myself. Not for a boss or for a corporation."
> **—Jessica Liebeskind, a 20-something makeup artist**

The femininity of Supergirls comes into major play when they enter the office. Our society doesn't quite know what to make of powerful women, and frankly, powerful women don't know what to make of themselves.

Jennifer Crisafulli isn't your hyped-up, testosterone-injecting powerwoman. She's a pretty brunette who flipped out when her task went wrong on *The Apprentice.* Not the kind of woman you could picture hunting down and killing cute, little innocent foxes, right?

And my friend, who told me to reclaim my "balls," is one of my girliest friends who spends hours doing her makeup every day and believes in "feminine power."

So, why is there a push for very feminine women in positions of power to act like men? Being courageous or brave is often associated with having "balls." Therefore, women who want to be powerful—especially young women—have to make a choice regarding how they want to appear. Yolanda felt like she took on a more masculine role when she stepped into her work clothes . . . but can femininity be valued in the workplace?

The forecast doesn't look good: Victoria Brescoll, a post-doctoral scholar at Yale University, unearthed another aspect of office politics that keeps all Supergirls in a bind. Brescoll had volunteers watch a series of videos of job interviews and asked them to assign a rank and salary to the job candidates. In the first video, job candidates described how they felt about losing an account because a coworker was late for a meeting; the volunteers assigned a male candidate who was angry about losing the account with the most superior office position and highest salary ($38,000), followed by a female candidate who was sad, followed by a female candidate who was angry (who would only rake in $23,000). The second video was the same, except the job candidates revealed their current position as CEO or entry-level. Surprisingly, volunteers rated the woman who reacted angrily to losing the account as "incompetent," even when they learned that she was the CEO and outranked the angry man. The volunteers felt that the male candidates, regardless of their anger, should earn over $70,000. They also felt that the women candidates who didn't express anger should earn $55,000, while the angry ones should earn about $32,000; the volunteers described the angry female candidates as "out of control."

Essentially, Supergirls aren't supposed to get angry. They can be bitchy, though. This is because "bitchy" is viewed as the manifestation of infantile frustration, which we understand as being possessed by high school girls, sorority sisters, and female coworkers on some kind of PMS-induced power trip. Anger, however, is for men.

Look at the obsession with "devil" magazine editors. A

bestselling book and a blockbuster movie—*The Devil Wears Prada*—were inspired by Anna Wintour, the editor of *Vogue*, being very difficult to work for. When Tina Brown's book *The Diana Chronicles* came out, much of the buzz focused almost exclusively on Brown being "self-absorbed" and a boss who favored men. Atoosa Rubenstein, the former editor of *Seventeen*, is known better in the media world for allegedly driving away half the *Seventeen* staff than for revitalizing the magazine's tone and brand. But all of these women have blazed new trails for women in magazine journalism, so perhaps the reason we are so obsessed with the "bitches" running magazines geared toward teen girls and young women is because that's the only industry where women have some control. Well, I'm not ready to take hookup tips and fashion advice from some scruffy male editors . . . are you?

There is a balance that can be struck. Half of it is pure and simple, according to author Hannah Seligson: "I would never tell people to be a bitch because I think it's a horrible management strategy." The other half is preserving your authenticity while adapting to the work culture, says Misha, a Supergirl University of Toronto grad who is now a biology research technician. "Recently, there's been a bit of drama at work . . . upon the arrival of one young woman from France, and things have just started going downhill. The whole lab seems to be engaged in some sort of silent battle. This young woman is extremely independent and intelligent, but she also can be a little stubborn and a little pushy. She's used to saying *"Mine, mine, mine!"* about her work, but when you work on a team, you have to start saying "our" about the work that everyone does together. She doesn't really seem to want to do things the way we do them. She gets defensive when she feels under attack, and everyone's mood is a little sour. . . . I think young women must observe how others in their work environment interact with their peers and adapt to that culture. [To do this] you just need lots and lots of meetings and discussions and communication."

Supergirls and the Pay Gap

Historically, women have always made less than men. As of 2004, the average woman made $30,724, while the average man made $40,668. According to the American Association of University Women, women make 75 cents for every dollar a man makes (and African-American women earn only 65 cents; Latina women, 53). And this pay gap seems to be widening, not decreasing . . . but isn't that bizarre in an age of Supergirls and powerful women?

The *Harvard Crimson,* Harvard University's student newspaper, found in a survey of 901 seniors in Harvard College's class of 2007 that the median starting salary for male students was $60,000; females, $50,000. The *Crimson* attributed the pay gap to several factors: "Part of the gap stems from the fact that males are more likely to enter lucrative sectors such as investment banking. Males also are more likely to graduate with degrees in economics, computer science, and other fields that are attractive to employers." But even controlling for industry sector and academic background, males appear to earn about 8 percent more than their female classmates, according to the *Crimson's* analysis. They found the greatest pay gap in the technology sector: "The median male salary in that industry is $74,000, compared to $50,000 for females."

A $24,000 pay gap!

Again, the *Crimson* identified two sources of the pay gap: women don't tend to enter male-dominated industries like banking, and they tend not to major in the lucrative areas of study that lead to these careers. Also, economists often cite that women don't ask for raises and responsibilities at the rate that men do, and women have children and often take time off to raise them, losing valuable time in the office (and, in fact, according to the Federal General Accountability Office, women with children take a 2.5 percent pay cut, while men with kids earn an extra 2 percent).

Also, women who ask for higher starting salaries and raises often have their reputations tarnished by their high aim. A 2007 study by Dr. Hannah Riley Bowles, an assistant professor at Harvard's Kennedy School of Government, found that when women do ask for raises, it hurts their reputation and likability. Dr. Riley Bowles had volunteers examining applications for a job where some of the applicants requested higher salaries; the volunteers felt less kindly toward the applicants who tried to negotiate, but the women who negotiated were viewed twice less favorably. In another part of the study, volunteers were asked to watch videos of applicants either applying for a job and being satisfied with the salary offered or applying for a job and requesting more money. The male volunteers said that they would not hire the women who negotiated for more money. The *Washington Post* wrote of the study, "Although it may well be true that women often hurt themselves by not trying to negotiate, this study found that women's reluctance was based on an entirely reasonable and accurate view of how they were likely to be treated if they did."

When we talk about women's earnings, it's also of immense importance to discuss "women's work." While generalizations aren't fun, it's fair to say that child care, education (especially in grade schools and high schools), and the nonprofit sectors are female-dominated fields. They are also *notoriously* underpaid fields. Coincidence? Probably not. Are women—even Super-girls—conditioned to take jobs in low-paying fields?

"It's hard to be working in nonprofit and education and get paid so little," says Erin, a 20-something from Chicago (when we spoke, Erin was temporarily stepping in as the executive director of a start-up nonprofit organization before starting to teach middle school in the fall). "My boyfriend and my best friend are both guys, and they are moving in together into a really nice apartment. They both have financial jobs and are smart, nice guys, but their résumés aren't astonishing, and I can't say I would trust either of them with a lot of money! Okay, so I am a little bitter: I worked like crazy in college, and my boyfriend is making three times as much as I am."

We also have to consider to what extent women—even overachieving young women—are conditioned to enter woman-dominated, low-paying fields. Erin, who is earning very little, actually had an early start in business. "When I was 12, I started a business where I would design birthday parties for kids. I had designed these different themed parties, with decorations and cake and favors and entertainment, and parents could pay a fee and I would put on the party for them." Clearly, this is a great combination of Erin's love of children and enormous business savvy. So, now Erin works with children . . . but the business component of her talents is not being utilized. But I bet that if Erin were a guy, one of her teachers or one of the adults she knew would have said along the way, "Wow, you have amazing business talent! You should really pursue this!" Chick lit books almost always feature young women working in the media, which have notoriously low starting salaries, whereas similarly glamorous books aimed toward young men, like Dana Vachon's *Mergers and Acquisitions* and David Bledin's *Bank,* depict banking, where starting salaries are almost always upward (well upward!) of $50,000.

Others feel that many overachievers try to steer clear of more thankless industries. "I have this sense that the people who are real overachievers don't go into journalism," says Garance Franke-Ruta, the online politics editor at the *Washington Post*. "The people I knew from Harvard who were the biggest overachievers tended to go in the direction of a regulated environment where achievement was met with certain awards and income. . . . Like, if you worked hard, you could go into medicine or law and succeed and almost automatically make money, whereas the overachievers don't seem as drawn to print journalism, because in general, it doesn't pay."

> "I worked like crazy in college, and my boyfriend is making three times as much as I am."
> —Erin, age 22

So why would Supergirls navigate toward low-paying careers? Part of it is likely because women are conditioned to gravitate toward "women's careers" and "women's majors." But the other reality is that we don't value children's education, social work, or care for the elderly; nor do we compensate it rightfully because it is "women's work."

"These are called 'feminized industries,'" says Hannah Seligson, author of *New Girl on the Job: Advice from the Trenches*, speaking of the industries like education, social work, nursing, and child care, where women employees are the vast majority. "They are compensated less because they are woman dominated, and the men who choose to enter these fields get rewarded with a higher salary and are promoted more quickly." Says Cathy Wasserman, an executive coach, "And, we're still seeing that even in the nonprofit field and other fields dominated by women that the number of male executive directors is absolutely out of proportion to the small number of men in the industry."

But it's not equality if women go into law for the sake of not being discriminated against as educators or in the nonprofit sector. In fact, many feminists, one of them Leslie Bennetts, author of *The Feminine Mistake*, take issue with the concept of avoiding feminized industries, because that's a Band-Aid to cover the bullet hole. Women need to be compensated equally and appropriately in whatever industries they choose. Period.

But it's not like the 20s are a total downer: even though Erin, the former UChicago Supergirl, is having trouble on the financial end, she's excited about her 20s. "I'm definitely not buying throw pillows—no money for that. However, it's great to be young and healthy and be able to travel. I love music, I love going to shows, and it's nice to sit on the couch at the end of the day and read for pleasure. You don't get to do that in college."

Some of the Supergirl traits that made young women flourish (well, "flourish") in high school and college don't serve them well in the real world. However, perhaps the 20s is the perfect time for young women to develop some authenticity that wasn't valued so much in high school or college. In the 20s (as I'm discovering right now), what happens with your career seems to be less a matter of how many hours you work—the key to success in high school and college—and more a matter of how those you interact with professionally perceive you . . . and that's where being warm and funny and authentic are really important. It's the first time that friends aren't automatically there—you have to work to meet people and make friends of your own volition, but it's impossible to develop relationships with others if you don't have a solid understanding of who you are. Plus, the twenties are a huge transition. When I was getting my first apartment and moving in with friends, I was *terrified*: Did this mean the end of my youth? After thinking about it, I realized that I was nervous about developing an identity outside of that of my family and my town and my old life . . . yet I felt like it was really time to step up to the plate and experience what life had to offer. So far, things have been going—knock on wood—really well!

And maybe things are changing. A 1999 *New York* magazine article about the rise of chick lit books for 30-something women hinted that perhaps getting older isn't so scary: "Coming of age is *nothing*," Elizabeth Kaplan, the New York literary agent, told *New York's* reporter. "*Being* of age is where it gets interesting." So perhaps Supergirls could make that work. If young women can work at a reasonable pace and take it easy in their 20s, getting older could be a lot of fun. After all, there's more up for grabs: after age 25, you can rent cars, buy apartments, and adopt families of kittens (or, you know, have kids). And after age 35, women can take on the Oval Office. Yes, that is where things are going to get interesting . . . as long as we don't shy away from our smarts and do take on our mental and emotional demons, woman-to-woman.

chapter five

"Do You Like My Hair?"

Supergirls Are Hot . . . at a Cost

*In order to be successful, one must project
an image of success at all times.*
—American Beauty

Supergirls are generally, well, hot. They seem to put an im
mense amount of energy into their appearance, whether it is
their hair, their clothes, their makeup/skin tone, or even how
composed or put-together they look, because on some level,
they know that as young women, brains can only take them
so far. The question arises if a girl can even be considered an
overachiever or a Supergirl if she is ugly (after all, aren't average-
looking intellectuals just considered nerds?), but how sexist is
that—that young women's beauty is such a prominent factor in
their success! The disservice that some young women do to their
bodies physically—from tanning to dyeing their hair (although
not officially dangerous but tell that to my tortured tresses) to
smoking—meshes perfectly with the disservice they do to their

bodies in their Supergirl activities . . . ingesting too much caffeine, not sleeping enough, and not giving their brains enough time to relax.

And this is largely where Supergirls' mental and physical breakdowns originate: not allowing themselves to get tired and hungry and burned out, and subsequently allowing their bodies to short circuit. It's not that they intentionally want to have a breakdown and be hospitalized for exhaustion, but rather, many young women simply pay little attention to their physical and emotional needs, as they want to do as much as possible without being slowed down by their bodies. But then again, maybe the inhuman amount of work they expect themselves to do without rest could be a little intentional flirting with a breakdown; it's sort of like the kids who don't hide their drug stash (whether it's weed or Adderall) because they secretly want to get caught, to have someone tell them "Stop!" As such, because of their constant working and overmedicating (whether it's with awards, caffeine, study, drugs, or Prozac), young women don't develop the "internal muscles"—the emotional strength to deal with problems that developes only from facing problems head-on in the past—that help them in times of trial . . . and they can't deal when things don't go their way.

Pegah, Age 15, Valley Stream North High School

Before I even met Pegah, I was warned by one of her close friends of one of Pegah's bizarre style idiosyncrasies: "She wears a size six shoe, but she's actually a size seven. She just doesn't want to be a size seven," her friend told me. "It's just that she wants to be perfect—and look it—at all times."

And she does. Pegah has long brown hair with delicate waves and highlights, glowing skin, big brown doe eyes, a nice nose, and a pretty smile with perfect pearly teeth. By society's standards, she has the perfect body: she's very thin and obviously has a small frame, but she's starting to fill out with the curves that come with being 15. Plus, she has the perfect clothes to accentuate it; her fashions are modest (no laces, deep V-necks, or excessively short skirts here), but it doesn't take a "skank tank" to make it clear that she's attractive.

"I spend about an hour every night picking out my entire outfit for the next school day," Pegah tells me. "I'll lay it out and look at everything and make sure it's perfect. I like looking really nice." In her room, she has baskets of makeup and cosmetics that are organized in blue and beige striped fabric drawers. When she blinks, you can see that she has three different shades of brown eye shadow on (Pegah also lays out her makeup palates the night before). However, occasionally Pegah does take the nice appearance thing a little further than you average perfect girl: "Our school has spirit week every year where there is retro day, mix and match day—where you're supposed to dress with, like, one color shirt and a totally different-colored bag, and pants and shoes and accessories that don't match at all—and twin day, and all these other silly themed days, and my friends all knew that I wouldn't participate. And, I mean, they were right. Why would I come to school looking so ridiculous?"

Pegah's stack of _Seventeen_'s and _InStyle_'s and her love of fashion can be deceiving: as much as she gets pleasure from assembling chic outfits and doing her hair and makeup, she is quite conscious of the sexist undertones regarding beauty in American society.

"There is just this constant expectation that girls should be pretty. Like, guys, they can be really hot if they just put on a T-shirt and jeans and go to school. However, for girls, they have to think so much about how they look and put all this effort into it. If there's one girl who guys want to date, she's the one who clearly puts hours into how she looks. And the other problem is, the second you start to become pretty, people think you're dumb or they assume you're less smart. It's like, if you're nice to look at, you're just eye candy."

What was interesting, though, is as we spoke, Pegah's intensity significantly flared; she stopped twirling the ends of her hair and started motioning with her hands and sat up straighter. "Women are only considered important for their looks: 99.9 percent of guys don't care how smart you are. Obviously, they would prefer a girl who is successful and impressive—and there are a few really nice guys who don't care how you look—but most would much rather have a hot girl. Guys grow up learning to want these girls who are insanely skinny, have huge boobs, nice skin, pretty hair, dress nicely, and all of that stuff that we're taught is beauty. And because so many girls want nothing more than a boyfriend, they are held to these awful expectations if they just want to be loved. It's like, if they want that validation, they have to be like models . . . but it's so hard for me, because I don't fit these standards."

This is difficult to hear, not only because I'm saddened by the cynicism and depressed concept of what one of today's most impressive young women feels guys want, but it's also puzzling because Pegah is, frankly, *stunning* . . . and she doesn't see it! "I don't think I'm pretty at all," she says simply, shrugging her thin shoulders. "I have this one friend, *she's* the hot one who all the guys like. But I'm just . . . *me*." But as she says this, her long eyelashes kiss in a blink and she smiles a little, and she is just striking!

"I want a nose job. I asked my mom about it, and at first she was really upset and almost offended that I'd want to change my nose, but then I kept bothering her about it more, and she said that if I wanted one, I could get one, but it would have to be after I moved out and went to college." Pegah also says that she dislikes her facial structure—"it's too round, and I wish I had higher cheekbones"—and I sadly wonder if that is not as much a by-product of girls being raised to hate their bodies, but rather the token Persian girl in a mostly white community sorting out the standards for beauty. Plus, her nice nose is one of the first things I noticed about her appearance.

Unfortunately, Pegah's sense of insecurity isn't just limited to her body: it's also in her brain. "I've recently been diagnosed with anxiety, but I'm not—and don't want to be—on medication. I've read so much about people getting addicted to prescriptions that I'm not willing to take that risk. And I kind of want to be able to work this problem out on my own . . . to fix what's really at the heart of why I'm so panicked all the time." Her doctor told her that she's at the level right now where she can probably manage her stress herself, but recommended that she take medication during midterms and finals when she becomes so gripped by fear that she can't do much outside of studying without getting panicky. "But I probably won't take it anyway," Pegah admits. This is despite the fact that Pegah comes home after school every day and works for a few hours at the desk in her kitchen, eats dinner, then goes upstairs to work until late at night, and gets "really shaky and freaked out if I stop to watch TV or something. I can't enjoy relaxing when I have even a possibility of work to do."

> "I've recently been diagnosed with anxiety, but I'm not—and don't want to be—on medication."
> **—Pegah, age 15**

The insecurity and fear that Pegah experiences is a big contrast to the girl who eats lunch at a local pizzeria with her friends and appears to be the leader of the group when they want to figure out where they should stand in the hall and what to do after school. "When I'm with my friends, I'm a completely different person. They're a huge source of support for me and they give great advice . . . but I don't like talking about my problems with them. I prefer to sort of have my time with my friends as a way to escape being so worried."

It's when Pegah is alone with her thoughts that things start to get uncomfortable. "It's when I'm home alone after school that I start to lose it. Sometimes I worry so much that I get physically dizzy and my mind starts to spin. I get nervous and anxious, and I start to worry about things that won't affect me for another ten years, like how I'll score on the MCATs." Literally, almost ten years away. "I don't know why I'm so strangled all the time and I hate it . . . but I feel like, to a certain extent, that's just me and how I get the most work done."

This situation isn't a total downer. Pegah isn't just book smart but also insightful: "It's when society agrees that girls—women—are good enough and shouldn't be judged by their looks that as individuals we'll be able to enjoy ourselves and enjoy our bodies more . . . but until then, it's hard to like yourself on your own because you're fighting this force individually, and the views of society and the media are really working against you." She has a nice blend of left-brain intellect and right-brain creativity; because of her possible ambitions of interior design, she has a fun patterned bedspread and perfectly arranged furniture that she picked out herself, her Vera Wang Princess perfume and other baubles arranged on pretty end tables, and a large framed poster of Audrey Hepburn in *Breakfast at Tiffany's* hanging above her bed. Pegah emanates this kind of contagious energy that makes you talk louder and faster when you speak with her; conversations with her eventually gain this almost hysterical momentum because her passion inspires the same sentiments in those she interacts with.

I hope, through the trajectory of Pegah's life, that she is able to keep up with herself, because she has some amazing ideas and great vision. I just hope the grip that society has on her beauty—both physically and emotionally—doesn't take her out first.

Perfect Beauty

I covered a county fair beauty pageant for a small community newspaper when I was in high school. One of the beauty pageant contestants I met with was a charming, very pretty 16-year-old enrolled in a local high school. She was telling me about the interview process of the pageant that took place a few days earlier.

"The judges asked questions about school and your interests and why you wanted to join the pageant," she told me confidently.

"Why did you want to join the pageant?" I asked her.

"I want to disprove stereotypes about beauty queens because," she said, looking down, "I'm not your average beauty pageant contestant."

I was puzzled: this young woman was friendly, thin, and white, with shiny brown hair, poise, and, well, disproportionately large breasts.

"How so?" I asked, trying to mask my confusion.

"Well, I'm *not tall*," she said.

This young woman presented her "deficiency" as some kind of really negative disadvantage that made me discreetly skim her appearance, looking for a prosthetic leg or third eye in the middle of her forehead hidden under a layer of foundation. But no, she was your standard thin, beautiful, big-breasted, poised beauty queen, who acted as though she was an awkward kid in sweatpants and orthodontic headgear just because she didn't tower over her average-height counterparts.

One of the most unusual things I've noticed about Supergirls is how much energy they put into their appearance. Nearly every single Supergirl I met with looked polished enough to be on the cover of *Vanity Fair*. America has strict standards of beauty: thinness, blonde hair, fair skin, discreet curves, clean facial features, and broader daintiness are highly rewarded. Those who don't comply are why the diet and plastic surgery industries are so flowering as of late.

However, the standards of beauty shape-shift among different cultures. Says Bahar, a college student who is of Iranian descent living in Texas, "There is always this notion that Persian girls are so pretty. So if you're labeled as a certain ethnicity and they label you as pretty, you don't want to be the exception to the rule. . . . I'm relatively fair and I have greenish eyes, and people look at that very favorably." What's fascinating, however, is that Bahar details that by Middle Eastern standards, being thin isn't as important as having a beautiful face. "By American standards of beauty, one can be tall and thin and maybe even have a kind of ugly face but still be beautiful. But the face . . . it's huge for us! Nose jobs and other plastic surgeries are common because you want to have the perfect facial structure if you want people to like you."

"Girls' beauty is of ultimate importance," Rachel, a teenager from upstate New York, told me. "So, if a girl—even if she's totally high-achieving and headed to Yale or whatever—is getting pale and she has to choose between studying for a test tomorrow or going tanning, she doesn't. She goes tanning first, then stays up extra late studying. Girls in high school know how important their looks are, and when you look at high school culture, girls are way more rewarded for being pretty than being smart. But if you can't get the credit you deserve for being smart, you might as well be recognized for being pretty and popular and sexy. Lots of successful girls would rather be hot than smart. Look at *Cosmopolitan* magazine: every month they run hundreds of pictures of beautiful, scantily clad women, and once every four issues or something, they'll run one little thing about a neurosurgeon or something."

Says psychologist Dr. SuEllen Hampkins: "Many women have this feeling that if they want to be loved, they have to have physical perfection of beauty. It's really clear that businesses stand to make a huge amount of money into inducing young women into feeling that they aren't perfect . . . but that they should buy physical perfection, whether it's diets, makeup, clothing, or plastic surgery." In our beauty-obsessed media culture, the rise of shows like *America's Next Top Model, I Want a Famous Face,* and *Extreme Makeover* make young women feel like "before" versions of themselves.

Says Allison, an upstate New York high schooler: "Look at the media nowadays! Look at all the stupid shows on TV, *The Hills, Laguna Beach,* and *The Simple Life:* there is this example set forth of blonde, beautiful girls who practically *say,* 'You have to be stick thin, have beautiful straight hair, say all the right things at the right time, and even if you like to act dumb, you need to have a great internship or a great job or a lot of money.' And these girls look so perfect! But I guess the thing we have to recognize is that while it looks like they are so natural and so effortless, they have clothes picked out for them and have people working on their hair and makeup for hours each day, and it's *not* a natural thing."

> "People pay more attention to beautiful women."
> **—Danielle, age 21**

And often these beauty processes are excruciating. I have a friend who gets regular Brazilian waxes, even though she has to go through the humiliation of having a perfect stranger working on her butt crack. Another friend of mine smells like bleach for two days after she gets her hair dyed blonde. And the other day, my tanning salon had some sort of promotion where if you come after 5pm and buy a lotion packet, you can go for free in their super-super-turbo bed. As I was laying in this contraption that essentially looked like an ultraviolet iron lung with bright purple lights that lined the inside of the bed and made your skin burn like crazy (and, for future reference, turn instantly bronze, unlike my spray tans, which sometimes give orange results), I thought to myself, *In the future, when we really respect women's bodies, this tanning bed will be considered some kind of patriarchal torture device.* What's so interesting is that my friends and I are all upwardly mobile girls, putting so much time and energy into how we look.

To further delve into this inherent double standard, in 2005 *Playgirl* surveyed their women readers and found that the majority were turned off by guys with perfect bodies and beauty routines: 73 percent of women said they wanted to see guys who were a little "rough around the edges," and 42 percent of the 2,000 women polled even indicated that they found love handles on men to be a turn-on! Compared with the models in *Playboy,* who often are so hand-selected and airbrushed that they don't even look *human,* this double standard indicates that there is definitely something going on with gender roles in this beauty mystique.

The Hot Factor

When we were younger, people would also assume that my token "hot friend" was dumb. She's relatively tall, she's skinny, she has shiny brown hair that is always perfectly blown out and curled at the ends, and her wardrobe is carefully compiled with pieces from American Eagle, Abercrombie, and North Face. People are sometimes surprised to learn that she has a 4.0 GPA in school, leads lots of clubs, and is a textbook Supergirl.

Danica McKellar, the television actress and author of *Math Doesn't Suck,* experienced similar discrimination in high school. "In the ninth grade in my science class, I used to wear brightly colored earrings and I was very outgoing, and the teacher said she was surprised that I got an A. 'I didn't think you'd be gifted at science,' she told me. 'You wear such brightly colored earrings!' It was like, in order to be smart, I had to be some sort of nerd, or that my fashion choices would take away from my skills. It was definitely discouraging."

We live in a sexist society that, to succeed, even the strongest, best-intentioned young woman has to appeal to the standards that she contradicts to make her voice heard and succeed. Even if a young woman wants to be taken seriously and respected, she has to be hot first, which automatically makes her taken less seriously.

"It's all based in this idea that a woman's contribution to society is to look good," says Amber Madison, who began writing her book, *Hooking Up: A Girl's Guide to Sex and Sexuality,* when she was a college junior and had it published when she was 22. "Whenever I go on a radio show, the DJ's first comment is always, 'You wrote a book about sex? You must be pretty hot,' or, 'I saw your picture. I'm glad I'm talking to you about sex.' It's never, 'Wow, you started to write this book in college? That's impressive!'"

"Similarly," Madison explains, "my boyfriend and I were watching TV the other day, and he made a comment about this one actress being hot, and I felt really, really threatened. And I was thinking, 'If he told me that he had read about a teenaged Olympic gold medalist, it wouldn't be nearly as threatening to hear.' I think it's ingrained in us to base our own judgment about women on their looks. And even if you're conscious of it, it's still something that's hard to get around."

So, Supergirls are hypersuccessful women, but a piece of their success is based on their looks. So how do they feel about the idea that the attractiveness of someone's body is a widely agreed-upon tool in scoring a young woman's success?

Slighted . . . but they go along with it. Says Danielle, a college student from a suburb of Sacramento, California, studying sociology: "There is definitely some power in being beautiful: psychologically, people pay more attention to beautiful women; people want to talk to them more, and they get extra time and attention paid to them at job interviews. And, of course, there's more gravitation toward beautiful women. . . . I mean, that's what our society really prizes women for."

Unfortunately, there is often a disconnect between young women being beautiful and being taken seriously: I know Anna Kournikova is a famous tennis player . . . but I know much more about how she looks and who she dates. When Condoleezza Rice wore knee-high leather boots on a trip to Germany, several major media outlets devoted entire articles to talking about her outfits. Once, a popular girl in my school used the word *circumlocution* at a meeting, and it was all people talked about at school the next day . . . that the pretty, presumably dumb girl had used the word *circumlocution*. Little did they know that she went on to attend one of the better SUNY schools.

To play devil's advocate for a moment, it's no surprise that people assume pretty young women are dumb. When I was a senior in high school, I had a friend with unnaturally tan skin, freakishly white teeth, highlighter blonde hair that she straightened for an hour when she wanted it flat, and a daily out-fit of a miniskirt with a sheer tank top. One day, she confessed to me that she was hurt that everyone thought she was stupid because of how she looked, when she actually had a near-perfect GPA. And frankly, I, too, had assumed she was dumb when I first met her . . . *because she "looked" dumb!*

The standards of beauty in our society—what we tell young women they should look like—do not simultaneously project an image of being intelligent or powerful. Hillary Clinton has taken a lot of crap for her wardrobe over the years, especially with her headbands that she wore during her husband's presidency, which perhaps were perceived as unprofessional . . . but can you imagine the extent to which people would ignore her if she was hunched over all the time, wearing tight sweater tunics, black leggings, and UGGs, or button-down shirts, wide belts, and miniskirts like today's high schools girls do?

But that's part of the huge catch-22: something that I became increasingly conscious of as I wrote this book is how a woman's beauty is factored into being an overachiever. To be an overachiev-ing guy, "Jimmy" can be a pasty nerd with blackheads who spends every Saturday night in college holed away in his cinder-block dorm room perfecting bio labs to graduate summa cum laude, and he would be fawned over by relatives at a family reunion. However, to be an overachieving woman, looks are imperative. If a young woman showed up to a family reunion, just having graduated from an Ivy League school with law school acceptances and an activi-ties résumé that couldn't fit on a roll of toilet paper, but she also had blackheads and pasty skin, we'd consider her a "brain" or "a genius." But no one would adulate her as a girl "doing it all" or as an overachiever, because she's not that put together, looks-wise. Technically, if she's not making time for exfoliation, salon appoint-ments, and tanning, she's not doing it all. Which sets us back to our original question: Why do girls have to be everything?

Yet sometimes being pretty *is* enough for young women to be accepted: in August 2007, Miss Teen South Carolina *totally* screwed up her interview question in the Miss Teen USA pageant, throwing in random references to "the Iraq" and South Africa in a question about why one-fifth of Americans can't locate the United States on a map.

Her answer: "I personally believe the U.S. Americans are unable to do so because, uh, some, uh . . . people out there in our nation don't have maps, and, uh, I believe that our education like such as South Africa and, uh, the Iraq everywhere like, such as and . . . I believe that they should, our education over here in the U.S. should help the U.S., err, uh, should help South Africa and should help the Iraq and the Asian countries, so we will be able to build up our future for our . . ."

She just babbled . . . but she looked great in an evening gown and hot in a swimsuit, so even though she completely bombed the "talking" and "thinking" portion of the competition, she placed *third*! What are we supposed to take away from that—act as though you've been lobotomized and you can still be successful if you're attractive?

If we're raising girls in a society where we tell them that it's hot to be smart, but Miss Teen South Carolina gets third place in her pageant and publicity spots on the *Today* show, then why don't young women just off themselves now?

The Relationship Between Beauty and Breakdowns

As I was working on this chapter, I read a startling news article about the rise of suicides among young women. According to a September 6, 2007, Reuters article, "In 2004, 4,599 children and adults aged 10 to 24 committed suicide, the biggest rise in suicides in 15 years. Suicide was the third-leading cause of death in that age group, the U.S. Centers for Disease Control and Prevention said. The increase was seen mostly in girls aged 10 to 19 . . . the biggest increase was among girls aged 10 to 14, where rates rose nearly 80 percent." Not to sound melodramatic, but I really feel like this has to do with the Supergirl dilemma. Because, honestly, during nights of endless AP homework where girls are so tired it hurts their eyes or during a week when friends and family members don't respond positively to girls' ongoing efforts to please everyone . . . well, who hasn't thought about killing herself? But that's at the end of a long trajectory that starts with our "caffeinated culture."

Says Cathy Wasserman, a New York–based career and life coach: "I think we live in this caffeinated culture—which doesn't necessarily just mean that we drink a lot of coffee—but that we're constantly going and going and doing and doing, trying to be perfect, and there is enormous pressure to keep that all up, which keeps you from relaxing and really settling into and discovering yourself and your intrinsic worth. . . . Many young women literally can't physically slow down, and sometimes it gets to the point that their bodies are trying to have an anxiety attack, but they are so dislocated from

> "I remember not wanting to go to the prom and dances because they were so expensive and it was such a meat market the way it objectified women. Girls were expected to have their nails, makeup, and hair done and buy a $500 to $2,000 dress, plus shoes, *plus* an after-party outfit. It was just like, *this is what is expected of girls:* to be pretty and materialistic."
> **—Erin, age 22**

themselves that they build a tolerance for it and are not fully aware of what's happening to them and the ill affects on their physical and mental health. Obviously, it's really dangerous!"

Says Jennifer, a graduate student at UC–Berkeley: "I like staying busy. Much of my sense of self is wrapped up in being a busy person. . . . I got tagged with this role, and once you sort of assume it, the expectations are always there and you really internalize them. I kind of expect this certain standard of busyness to be *me*, even if it has negative effects."

Probably the most drastic side effect of neglecting your health is a breakdown. Provided the entire Supergirl population doesn't experience mass burnout, they are likely to become tomorrow's astronauts, CEOs, and presidents. But they might have some interesting stories beforehand about what happens when people don't give their bodies a rest. "This culture of overachieving makes many young women very mentally and emotionally unstable," says Dr. SuEllen Hampkins, the former Smith College psychologist.

In fact, when pressed, many of the Supergirls I spoke with admitted to having a breakdown in some sense of the word. Morgan, who attended high school in suburban Colorado, had a breakdown that was systematic of overscheduling and family problems. "I was in a high school that wasn't all-around competitive, but it had an incredibly competitive top 10 percent that experienced this huge push to do everything; so I did . . . I was in art, photography, journalism, the debate team, and AP classes." But when her dad was diagnosed with Parkinson's disease, Morgan couldn't take it. "I had a huge breakdown: I couldn't breathe! I started hyperventilating and was panicking, and I had to go to the hospital because I just couldn't calm down."

Justine, a hyperachieving Supergirl at UC–Berkeley, had been in the middle of giving a talk about being a Pacific Islander to a large group of UC–Berkeley students. "And the students were asking me all sorts of questions about Pacific Islanders and how they felt about certain issues, and I was like, *I can't speak for all the thousands of Pacific Islanders!* And I just started freaking out, and it really didn't have much to do with the talk but just from having all this pressure in my life, and I started hysterically crying and ran out of the room. Luckily, my mentor, who had been in the room, followed me outside and urged me to sort of get it together and turn this into a learning experience. So I went back inside and explained to everyone the kind of pressures I was under and why I broke down . . . so I hope I was able to make my outburst into a learning experience."

Often, these breakdowns can be hugely helpful. Some young women use work, alcohol, and medication to keep going, but sometimes the breakdowns motivate them to get in touch with themselves and what their needs actually are . . . rather than continuing to hang on by a string like how children's half-dead baby teeth dangle by fleshy cords. Says Cathy Wasserman: "When you face the pain and limitations of your humanity and your struggles, there is a wisdom and maturity that come with it. Some young women are missing coming face-to-face with that and face-to-face with themselves."

Unfortunately, this sentiment of being owned by the Supergirl reputation—a sentiment possessed by many of the Supergirls I spoke with can often get totally blown out of proportion when girls take society's messages on women's devaluation truly to heart. "I had a client who came to me and we were talking about the concept of intrinsic worth, which is what a person contributes to the world that doesn't have to do with their accomplishments or community service or salary; it's just who they are," says Wasserman. "And when we talked, she told me that she wasn't sure that she had intrinsic worth. So she went home and talked to some of her friends, and when she came back the next week, she said that some of her friends did think that they had a solid sense of intrinsic worth but that she wasn't so sure. She just wasn't positive that she had worth outside of her accomplishments."

Anna Quindlen, a *Newsweek* columnist and famous author, wrote in her recent book *Being Perfect*, "What is really hard, and really amazing, is giving up on being perfect and beginning the world of becoming yourself. . . . But this is worse: someday, sometime, you will be sitting somewhere . . . and something bad will have happened: you will have lost someone you loved, or failed at something at which you badly wanted to succeed. And sitting there, you will fall into the center of yourself. You will look for some core to sustain you. And if you have been perfect all your life and have managed to meet all the expectations of your family, your friends, your community, your society, chances are excellent that there will be a black hole where that core ought to be."

While this advice feels a touch disingenuous from a woman who went to Barnard and has experienced one of the most successful careers in journalism of women in our time, I personally can really identify with this. My junior year of college, I made the mistake of transferring away from my small liberal arts college in lower Manhattan, where kids were creative and unique and hilarious . . . but some weren't so hot on studying, being registered to vote, or knowing who their state's governor is, and I felt like they took down the rest of the group. So in the fall, I skipped off to SUNY–Stony Brook, a public school in a somewhat rural part of Long Island that claimed to have rigorous standards for admission and nice scenery near the Hamptons. Their admissions brochures showed preppy kids in polo shirts flashing their perfect teeth, smiling and laughing, and I had visions of drinking

Long Island iced teas at parties with my preppy friends . . . but when I got there, it was all inverted engineering majors (with unapologetically bad teeth) who thought my bubbliness was a disease. The classes were huge, boring, and not as academically rigorous as I'd hoped. The school was apparently nowhere near the Hamptons, and people didn't even drink! I had virtually no friends, and I had to take the public bus into town every time I wanted to go tanning or go to Duane Reade or get Starbucks (and almost every time, I got stranded in town in the rain). I had never been so lost before in my life . . . and I didn't have that inner sense of self, that "internal muscle" to sustain me. I felt like I was constantly one minor annoyance away from a break-down. After all, I had spent pretty much my entire adolescence trying to be accomplished, liked, and people-pleasing . . . but because of that, I had no clue why I mattered, because my worth always depended on being around others and others' approval.

So I did the only thing I knew to do: I split my time between Manhattan and Stony Brook for the remainder of the semester and moved back to the city in the spring, returning to my friends and, yes, my old school. Being at Stony Brook (and recovering from Stony Brook!) was definitely the hardest six months of my life, and because there were no liquor stores, no eligible guys to hook up with, and virtually no other outlets for destructive be-havior to take my stress out on, I had to come face-to-face with myself and admit to myself that I had been living really inau-thentically for years. I spent the winter break after the semester relaxing and meditating and painting—and trying to figure out why I mattered—but a lot of finding myself was in moving back to New York and going back to my old life of going on dates, going to book parties, and doing networking lunches that make me feel important and like I'm in control.

I, too, am a work in progress.

When we think of young women who hate themselves and take it out on their bodies, we don't automatically think of young women working eighty hours a week between school and studying and work and clubs. But isn't the sleeplessness, the OD-ing on caffeine, and the complete ignoring of the body's needs a type of self-abuse? When we think of girls needing "control" and finding control in whatever way they can, we don't think of girls spending half an hour every morning picking out the perfect outfit, redoing their eyeliner until it's perfect, and staying crazy busy during the school day so that they don't have to think about how empty they feel—we think of anorexics and bulimics. But then again, who is to say that's not a problem, either?

chapter six

"I'm Not Hungry, Really!"

Supergirls Are Skinny . . .
by Any Means Necessary

....

I'm one stomach flu away from my goal weight.
—"Emily," the first assistant to "Miranda Priestly"
in the movie version of *The Devil Wears Prada*

The stereotype about young women with anorexia is more often than not unnervingly true: type-A, hyperambitious, control-loving young women are incredibly prone to the disease. However, Supergirls are also drawn to other eating disorders, like bulimia, exercise bulimia, and overeating . . . and a majority of young women deal with an amorphous disorder vaguely titled "disordered eating." Why? Because food can be withheld to help a person regain control in a world where nothing can guarantee admission to Harvard, where bosses can be demanding, and where "good" doesn't have a workable definition . . . but food can be spackle to temporarily fill the emptiness and provide a sense of reliability. Many young women today have been dieting since they were cognizant; they have no recollection of a time when they ate normally or liberally—or at least, not without feeling bad about it.

There is no hunger on earth like having an eating disorder, because absolutely nothing can satisfy it. Today's young women are raised to hate their bodies, yet, like blue ribbons and awards, sizes actually aren't good measures of people.

Leah, Age 18, the State University of New York at Albany

Leah is a pretty girl. I never once saw her without makeup, but she doesn't even really need it because she has high cheekbones, pretty eyes, and nice skin. She's not like the girls who you see around campus with their unseasonably tan hip bones peeking out of the top of their University at Albany sweatpants, practically stepping out of their UGG boots . . . Leah is, to put it delicately, curvaceous. She's not *fat* . . . she's just a little bigger than normal, when the "normal" standard that girls are held to is emaciated.

While Leah says that she feels comfortable in her skin, "It takes active effort to not get swept up in this eating culture," she concedes.

After all, it's obvious there are constant conflicting messages at UAlbany about food and fitness. There's food everywhere: each quad has at least one cafeteria, the student union boasts an entire floor full of food, and vending machines seem to be around every corner. The meal plan that students have is complicated; students have a certain number of "meal swipes" and an additional amount of flexible dollars on their meal plans, but after a certain time of day, any trip to the cafeteria can count as a meal plan swipe . . . which requires a lot of thinking and strategizing about what a student will eat that day. Plus, the food at UAlbany is really, really good, which although is nothing to hold against a school (hanging out with Leah was one of my favorite trips that I did for this book, if for no other reason, because there was the possibility of eating Au Bon Pain soup in a bread bowl for every meal of the day), it does make it easy to develop some disordered eating habits. Plus, because there is the meal plan swipe program, when you're paying $11 for a lunch, you want to make it worth your money, which is why Leah and I eat steak wraps, perogies, salads, and a cookie at lunch one day in a single meal.

And although Leah maintains that there isn't a dominant social group on campus—and there probably isn't—the stick-thin girls in tight jeans tucked into knee-high boots flitting by do set a certain standard of thinness, having fat in the right places, and beauty . . . and they get a lot of positive reinforcement for their looks by the campus community.

The UAlbany sororities started recruiting attractive pledges early; according to Leah, some of the top sororities combed through the members of Facebook groups like "UAlbany Class of 2011," "Albany Freshmen," and "You know you go to Albany when . . ." and invited incoming freshman girls whose pictures were becoming of their desired pledges to join "Hair color 'X' Sorority Rush 2007–08" groups on Facebook. One of Leah's friends, a tall, thin blonde, was invited by several sororities to consider pledging, during the summer before her freshman year . . . although the sororities never met her and just saw her pretty picture.

Similarly, there are several club-promoting Web sites that make it a point to go to Albany clubs and take pictures of the attractive (underage) Albany students for their Web sites . . . and more often than not, the pretty girls with straight hair holding amaretto sours in their hands and kissing one another's cheeks are the same girls strutting around campus embodying these standards of physical perfection for UAlbany women.

Leah herself is a prime eating disorder candidate. Her world is completely hyperorganized from the moment she wakes up in the morning: in fact, she has five different modes of schedule keeping. She has a day planner (University of Albany–issued, of course) that is color coded to indicate which items are tests or homework or meetings, and it is free of worn edges or crinkles (unlike my tortured, equally overworked day planner). Each day, she has a precise schedule for herself written on a vertical index card that details exactly where she has to be when; for example, she has her second class of the day listed as "Spanish: 11:20–12:10," which she promptly crosses off during lunch five minutes later. Her entire day is scripted like this. In fact, her entire week is: she makes her week's index cards on Sunday night and pins them to her bulletin board above her desk, and then clips the day's card in her agenda book every morning before she leaves her dorm. She has also made a spreadsheet in Microsoft Excel on her computer with the syllabi for her five classes that show, day by day, what will be covered in class and what's due; each day is newly highlighted in yellow. Leah also has another color-coded calendar on the wall and usually keeps one on her desk, but she "hasn't had the chance to make it up yet." Wonder why.

Leah concedes that all of her organizing—like writing down the minute details of where she has to be when and writing out extra note sheets for chapters that haven't been assigned for class—is often superfluous, and it kind of reminds me of how, as an anorexic, I would go crazy writing down every little thing I ate and how many calories it had.

"Although my schedule now doesn't allow for me to go to the

gym . . . I used to go every day during the summer, and I don't want to say that I'm slacking right now—because I'm running around campus doing work instead—but, you know, it's weird not having it as a part of my routine when it was such a big part of the summer." However, an interesting question arises here: Does Leah not work out and not diet because she has so much to do, or does she find so much to do because she feels like becoming thin is unachievable and she has to compensate by overachieving?

Either way, I feel really bad for Leah in her situation, because today's girls are raised in such a precarious limbo; craving thinness is a given and dieting is really hard (and statistically, success with dieting is unlikely). However, because of the teen media's obsession with talking about eating disorders and girls who have had eating disorders (and, interestingly enough, often in a more sensationalistic way than a cautioning way), girls know that they could be a few self-esteem pitfalls away from a long battle with anorexia or other eating disorders.

However, eating is elementary to living; fueling with calories is like sleeping to recharge, or even breathing in and out. So why are today's highest-achieving girls so obsessed with what they eat? Because our misogynistic society and media, desperate to remind girls of their limitations, have forced them to have a love/hate relationship with an element that they need to survive.

My Story

There are a few things that prevent me from being an all-out Supergirl: I'm late for things 80 percent of the time, and when I'm not, I probably made a mistake somewhere in my scheduling book and thought my appointment was ten minutes earlier than it actually was. I can be flaky (although this is more a by-product of taking on too much at one time). I have fervent opinions that I have trouble keeping to myself. And I'm overweight. Although all of these are unintended pockmarks that appeared after I was pried from the Supergirl plaster mold, the latter is in complete defiance of the Supergirl lifestyle.

But I dealt with anorexia, anorexia athletica (exercise addiction), and binge eating in high school. The thing I remember most about being anorexic is how cold you are. It's been five years and some details are fuzzy (some probably repressed), but I will never forget that feeling of being so freezing, like you'll never get warm again. I don't remember having a running addiction as being as bad as it actually was, because I was so souped up on exercise-induced endorphins . . . but it probably wasn't actually that much fun, because my muscles were *always* sore from running between five and eight miles every day during the height of my disorder. Binge eating is the worst of all, because despite what you'd think about the satisfaction of eating an entire batch of oatmeal cookies without thinking once about the calories, it's not even remotely fun. It's a protest.

Anorexic women are taught that they are being "good." We raise young women to really hate their bodies, and when someone finally becomes emaciated, she often feels like she is finally complying with societal norms to the fullest extent. When I was at my thinnest, during September 2002 through January 2003, I didn't really talk, and I never disagreed with anyone or said anything really contrary; I just wanted people to like me and to think I was good. Unfortunately, this hunger to be good was funneled entirely into my thinness; the thinner I got, the more "good" I felt. I remember a close friend once telling me, when I was nearly at my lowest weight, that I looked like a Holocaust survivor. I made a pouty face and looked away, but more to conceal my smiling inside: *"Finally!"* What was more interesting was that I didn't really want to be thinner at that point, I just wanted to weigh less. I knew when I was 90 pounds that you could count every rib in my back and that I looked terrible, but I wanted to weigh 88 pounds (8 is my favorite number). Not to mention, I've never received such positive feedback for anything I've done as I did for being thin.

But I don't blame anyone—in fact, I loved the positive reinforcement. It gave me all the more motivation to ignore my hunger pangs, thinning hair, and ribs protruding from my back. I strictly ate 600 calories a day . . . and wrote down the calorie counts of everything I ate. Friends and family members who knew about my obsessive counting would periodically ask me how many calories I had eaten that day or was generally eating, and I would become repulsed by their query; to me, how many calories I was eating was the equivalent of a sum that quantified for an adult his or her worth through a combination of his or her salary, likability, gender, race, hierarchy in the office, age, and sexual potency. It was my ultimate—and only—power.

Having an eating disorder also skewed the way I looked at my gender. When I was 85 pounds and had blood pressure of $^{70}/_{40}$ in the ninth grade, that was the year I decided math was useless, having a boyfriend meant you were "good," and Paris Hilton was cool. In fact, all through elementary school and middle school, I really liked math and wanted to be good at it . . . but it wasn't until I was anorexic that seeing a calculator conjured the same feeling in the pit of my stomach that the sight of a syringe at the doctor's office does for most people who fear shots.

But what was harder—although not necessarily as deadly— was dealing with a binge eating disorder. Part of why eating three turkey pitas, half a batch of oatmeal cookies, four bowls of cereal, and a half gallon of milk is such a struggle (and not just physically, trying to keep all that food down) is because it's not even remotely fun: it makes you feel stupid, ugly, gross, and bad. Eating so much makes you feel worthless, *especially* after considering your weight to be the ultimate measure of your worth for the past year.

Although I now have little-to-no inclination to eat entire bags of Reese's Peanut Butter Cups, I am still not totally comfortable in my skin. Plus, I can't help but think that my life would be radically different if I were thin; I get into these thought patterns like, "Would he have liked me back when I was thin?" "Would I have gotten that fashion magazine internship if I was skinny?" or "Would I have made friends more easily at my new school if I wore a size 0 again?"

When I actually was a size 0, few of my peers expressed distaste in my shriveling size; people were asking me for diet tips through the days that I started seeing black whenever I stood up. It takes energy, passion, and an austere dedication to self-deprivation to stop eating or to purge your food. By and large, we just don't want to confront these eating disorders . . . probably for the same reasons that we don't want to confront the Supergirl dilemma. Why stop an individual on her quest to perfection?

Because it's lethal.

Raised to Hate Their Bodies by Family, Friends, and the Media

When I was in the second grade, I told my teacher that I was on a diet. She looked down at me, somewhat incredulously.

"You're not on a diet. . . . 'Diet' isn't the right word. You're probably just trying to eat healthier, right?"

"No." I shook my little head, blonde curls bouncing. "My dad said I had to go on a *diet*. He said everyone in my family did."

I was seven. And at that ripe age, I understood that being on a diet was something standard that a young girl might do . . . except, perhaps not for girls *that* young.

> "I spent age 11 to 14 trying to lose . . . weight."
>
> **—Sasha, age 20**

Our society raises young women to hate their bodies. Although eating disorders and body image issues are most commonly associated with Beverly Hills teens and WASPy women from Westchester, these issues truly know no region or socioeconomic status. Says Maya, a senior at the prestigious Georgetown Day School: "In my group of seven best friends, four of us have suffered from full-blown eating disorders, and the rest of us have dealt with various forms of disordered eating." Liz from Revere High School in Massachusetts said that body image issues were of "huge" concern to her peers: "A lot of girls are too thin or anorexic, and obesity is a big problem, too. The students at my school just have constant problems with their size." This brings up the constant problem of disordered eating, which I'm comfortable asserting that every single American woman deals with to some degree.

Sasha, who grew up in California, dealt with food issues since she was a child because she took steroids for kidney failure and ended up becoming overweight. "So I spent age 11 to 14 trying to lose that weight. I didn't want to just not be overweight: I wanted to be really thin. . . . So I developed bulimia and ended up throwing up all the time. I was able to stop by the time I got to college, but unfortunately, my freshman 15 was more like the freshman 40. I was also dating one of the school football players at the time, and he was really bad for me. He would always tell me to stop wearing the clothes I wore, like, *'No one wants to see that,'* and would always throw his huge football jersey at me and say, *'You should be wearing this.'* So I started throwing up again, and this time it was a habit that was a lot harder to kick."

Samantha, the Supergirl from the Boston prep school who dealt with anorexia, was influenced by a friend with unhealthy habits . . . and ended up like gum on the bottom of her friend's shoe. "I had a friend freshman and sophomore year who was anorexic, bulimic, and cut herself . . . and I ended up essentially getting it from her. But although I had helped her through her disorder, when I was anorexic, she was like, 'I'm sorry, but I can't help you and be here for you. I honestly can't go through this again. . . . I can't do that to myself.'"

According to the National Eating Disorders Association (NEDA), there are at least ten million American women and one million American men suffering from anorexia and/or bulimia at any given time. There are also an estimated additional twenty-five million Americans suffering from overeating. The Renfrew Center Foundation for Eating Disorders' publication *Eating Disorders 101 Guide: A Summary of Issues, Statistics, and Resources* reports that eating disorders affect seventy million individuals worldwide, with Americans making up twenty-four million of those seventy million. The United States alone contributes over a third of the world's eating disorders sufferers; meanwhile, the United States barely makes up 5 percent of the world's population.

Why? In my opinion, fingers can be pointed at Manhattan and Hollywood, where so much of society's constructs of beauty are created. And apparently, I'm not alone in that conviction: Says Rachel, a high school student from upstate New York: "The media gives young people really screwed-up views on their bodies. Like, look at an Abercrombie ad: their models don't look like normal people. They're *perfect*. But the difference is that guys don't take this message to heart and feel like they have to immediately go to the gym after walking by wall-sized posters of really hot guys in an Abercrombie store, but girls see it as a reminder of their insecurities and a reminder of where they're not good enough, and they really take those images to heart."

The media inspires real fear over women's size, like *Jane* magazine (RIP) talking about women's "Buddha bellies," mothering magazines publishing new postbaby diets every month, and *Glamour* magazine publishing articles with workouts for women to get rid of their "muffin top," while running features on how to love your body or saying in their "It's Okay to . . ." monthly column: "It's okay to . . . have frozen yogurt for dinner!"

Yet, it really isn't okay to have frozen yogurt for dinner. That's really terrible for your body; what we need is an eating culture where it is okay to eat a sensible dinner and then have a normal portion of frozen yogurt for dessert. The media teaches young women to see very disordered eating habits as normal. In October 2007, *First* magazine advised readers to wear mittens on their hands while preparing for parties they were hosting and while hors'doeuvres were being served so that they wouldn't be tempted to eat before dinner . . . but honestly, if I saw someone at a party who was so emotionally crazed by food that she chose to wear mittens to keep her from eating what she desired, I'd be concerned for her randomly losing it and shooting everyone at the soiree. Lindsay Lohan once said that when she goes out for meals, when she feels as though she's eaten enough, she pours her drink over her food to keep her from eating more. And people listen to her! I was horrified recently when I saw a woman douse her pad thai with her iced coffee at my favorite noodle bistro in Manhattan.

Another paradox within the media is that magazines and celebrity TV news shows will run articles or air segments on which celebrities are "scary skinny" and will run "perky" profiles of teen girls who suffered from eating disorders, and then feature the said celebrities on the cover or on the show with the same eating disorder, discussing how they don't have eating disorders and that there is such pressure in Hollywood to be thin and that the populace is so critical—but they have a great body image and love to in-line skate and eat gummy bears. "The images of women in the media are thinner than ever, and popular women's magazines bemoan the fact that *so-and-so* has become anorexic, but she's still glamorous on the cover of the magazine or in ads three pages down," says psychologist Dr. SuEllen Hampkins.

(For the record, I was the subject of an article in *Teen People* in August 2005 on my struggle with anorexia and an exercise addiction; while the article came off as quite sympathetic and empowering for young women, this was in the same issue that Lindsay Lohan, in the beginning of her blonde and stick-thin phase, was on the cover, denying that she had an eating disorder and criticizing people for talking about her weight.)

Such genuine dislike of food and fat inherent in eating disorders is fueled by the diet industry, now a $60 billion industry. In the 2005 diet book *Skinny Bitch,* which spent several months at the top of the *New York Times* bestseller list, authors Rory Freedman and Kim Barnouin insist to readers that "Soda is liquid Satan," and the book has a chapter called "Sugar Is the Devil." I could understand heroin (or Goldschläger) garnering similar comparisons to Satan and the devil, but likening food to evil is not only downright stupid but downright dangerous.

There is nothing worse in our society than being a fat woman. In an argument, when a woman is called fat, she is at the end of her rope. You'll be okay if you're called a "bitch" and you'll make it if you're called a "fugly slut," but being called "fat" is something that takes time to recover from. In 2003, Kelly Osbourne told London's *Sunday Mirror,* "'It's so superficial and so stupid. . . . People look down on you more for [being overweight] than if you're a junkie or a thief. I think it's sick. Who says being skinny is even attractive?"

Our society considers overweight women to be less capable of doing good work and to be somewhat lazy. They are considered to be doomed to a life of loneliness and "otherness." Our society revels at the idea of lonely overweight women becoming vivacious upon losing weight: movies like *My Big Fat Greek Wedding* and books like *Secrets of a Former Fat Girl: How to Lose Two, Four (or More!) Dress Sizes—And Find Yourself Along the Way* illustrate how life opens up like daffodils in the spring when a fat woman starts shedding pounds.

The sexuality of overweight women is ignored and often feared. Bernie, the size 16 mannequin created for Saks Fifth Avenue, is consistently dressed in unfortunate sweater sets and mid-calf-length skirts, while her size 2 counterparts model lingerie, dresses with plunging necklines, and thong swimsuits. Movies like *Shallow Hal* and *Norbit* are intended to repulse viewers with the idea of a plus-sized woman wanting sex.

No wonder why today's young women are so terrified at the concept of eating: being overweight has implications of employers not wanting to hire you, people feeling sorry for you, and guys being repulsed by the idea of you wanting sex. While I personally would dissent how wholly realistic these fears are, sadly there is some truth to all stereotypes.

Supergirls Going Without Fuel

When she was in high school, Erin was *the* Supergirl. She was at the top of her class, led several clubs in school, and was extremely well liked by her peers. For all her life, Erin identified with feminism and "wouldn't even drink a diet Coke" for how it mainstreamed paranoia about fatness. She was conscious of how girls were encouraged to hate their bodies, and even though she was already fairly thin for her 5'8" athletic frame, she didn't put a ton of thought into her size. Until she randomly decided to go on a diet . . . a major diet that involved eating very little and running every day . . . just to see what would happen.

"Independence and intelligence only carried me so far, but dieting garnered me a ton of positive reinforcement," she says. After dropping weight, Erin had random strangers coming up to her in public to tell her how beautiful she was, which fueled her efforts to eat less and become thinner and thinner. "The response I got for being so thin was more affirmative than for any of the really large achievements I had gotten before that, like in school or with leadership activities. People were walking up to me on the street, saying, *You are the most beautiful woman I've ever seen.*'" When Erin's weight dipped to almost 100 pounds (keep in mind, Erin is 5'8"), she had three different modeling agents approach her about getting into the business. "I looked unnatural and scary, and people were approaching me to represent to other women what they should look like.

"In hindsight, I attribute most of the eating disorder that I developed to the fact that I was extremely uncomfortable being as smart and as high-achieving as I was. I had to prove that I was feminine. I had a male counterpart in high school who was, like me, the leader of everything, had straight A's, and was really well liked. It was cool for him to do that, but it wasn't cool for me to be so well rounded without compensating. . . . And it's this being a *girl* that teaches you that nothing you do is good enough. You are constantly in punishment mode, hating yourself."

Jordan, a twenty-three-year-old senior at the University of

Arizona unfortunately is more than familiar with how being a Supergirl can fuel eating disorder efforts. "I go to the gym a lot, usually for an hour and a half. I'm trying to find a bicycle so that can be my main transportation. I eat really healthy—a high-protein, low-carb diet." Jordan's seemingly strict diet and exercise regimen is the result of issues with weight that started when she was in middle school, when she had unconsciously put on a few pounds. "I don't know what it was that promoted my major weight gain when I was in middle school, but I wasn't aware of it until I got into a major fight. This girl who was popular came up to me and started saying really rude stuff to me, like I was a 'fat animal.' After that, I changed my eating habits and starting riding a bike to school. One of my cousins worked for a weight-loss clinic in California who introduced me to a high-protein, low-carbohydrate diet. In high school, it got a little out of hand; I was probably anorexic. My diet got to maybe 700 calories a day. I ate tuna and oranges for lunch and dinner, and cereal for breakfast." Jordan now recognizes that such meager food intake and the fact that she stopped getting her period are all symptoms of anorexia. "I'm still concerned, just because I've struggled so much with my eating habits, but I guess I'm not as concerned about my weight as I was back then in high school."

What makes Jordan's revelation even more telling, though, is that she thrives on schedules and regimens and boundaries. Her work and class schedule at school is busy-busy-busy, and she's "afraid of what my life is going to look like after school. I'm thinking about joining the Peace Corps or the military. I'm just the kind of person who needs structure. I'm taking the LSAT, probably going to law school." The parallels inherent in an anorexia survivor wanting to go to law school and join the military pretty much speak for themselves . . . eating disorders fester in those who need structure and a bit—or rather, a great deal—of austerity.

Similarly, there is an irony in that Supergirls, who need mental agility and physical endurance to *go-go-go!* at all hours of the day, are probably the least adequately fueled of all girls. The stories of high-achieving Supergirls like Erin were the subject of 27-year-old Courtney Martin's first book, *Perfect Girls, Starving Daughters: The Frightening New Normalcy of Hating Your Body.* In her book, Martin, who struggled with body image issues while in college and her 20s, takes on how normal it is for women to hate their bodies and why high-achieving women are so drawn to problems with food. She argues that a variety of factors, from family issues to societal misogyny, can spur eating disorders, but hoists a great deal of the blame for eating disorders on the pressures on young women today. What jumps out of the pages of this book is how much women use food as a measure for *control.*

Martin writes, "A cookie can suddenly take on the gargantuan meaning of a grade—if you avoid the sweet, comforting taste in your mouth at a boring meeting, you pass. If you are lazy, out of control, undisciplined and eat this wretched little concoction, you fail. There is nothing more disgusting to a perfect girl than the taste of failure." Certainly, there is much more to be absorbed in the 300 pages of Martin's book, but what jumps out over and over again is that eating is one thing that stays constant and can be controlled in young women's unpredictable, over-scheduled lives.

Sasha, the UC–Berkeley student, was able to get control of her struggle with bulimia by starting to work at the Gender

"Dieting is so ubiquitous. . . . It was rare to see people of above average weight on campus."

—former Smith College psychologist and author Dr. SuEllen Hampkins

Equity Center and planning programming for the campus's Love Your Body Week: she recognized that latching onto activism could help her recognize what went wrong for her and could help others before eating disorders got to them. Certainly, there are steps everyone can take (without necessarily getting all activist-y) to confront the eating disorders epidemic: holding the media accountable for the images of bodies they run, like fashion magazines running ads of models with bones protruding where bones shouldn't protrude or publishing alarmist articles on "muffin tops."

We also have to take a breather from freaking out over the obesity crisis and reevaluate why our society has such a weird relationship with food; we withhold food to feel loved, but isn't food also a cultural herald of warmth and love? Personally, I sense that until American society really evaluates why it vaunts this dichotomy of self-deprivation of the soul versus the indulgence in the material as cultural ideals, it will be impossible to genuinely love your body.

Something that really chilled me, a year or so ago, was my mother holding the newsletter for the National Eating Disorders Association in her hand and recommending that I join the organization: "Because NEDA does so much for research on eating disorders and for advocating for better and more affordable health care for eating disorder patients." She swallowed hard. "And you and I both are aware of the rate at which eating disorders surface again."

Although I like to think that I go easier on myself now than I did when I was anorexic five years ago, there are nights when I write and work until my eyelids are draping over my dry eyes and I feel like nothing I do will ever be *enough*. There are still days when I finish a long power walk or a session with the Stairmaster . . . and I want to go longer. And there are happy hours when

I feel pretty guilty about downing an order of chicken flautas and a margarita (or three). But I'm conscious of how our society raises young women to hate their bodies . . . and perhaps, if all young women were, there would be no need to preemptively join the National Eating Disorders Association.

But there's also another step to be taken, and it's a step that requires young women to really collectively examine their lives and examine how they pit themselves against other women. To be perfectly candid, I know when some people I've just met guess that I'm an unassuming overweight girl, and it's not until I do a little name-dropping, mention that I've written a book, or just flash my Tiffany bracelet that said people will stop talking about themselves as though they're *so interesting* and finally ask me about myself because, you know, I might actually be interesting. Being thin is currency—it's a calling card that touts self-control and success—and being overweight is just the opposite. People assume that perfection is a race and that those who are thin are already leaps and bounds ahead. But we need to figure out how we can stop adjudicating people by how much they do and how they look, and understand that either way, they matter. We need to erase some of this dog-eat-dog competitiveness from society and understand that trying to size up and compare people with superficial measures of their worth doesn't make anyone feel good about themselves.

But some think it does . . . and that is its own subject to be explored.

chapter seven

"She's Such a Bitch!"

Supergirls Can Be Competitive . . .
Even with Our Best Friends

Don't cha wish your girlfriend was hot like me?
—Pussycat Dolls

Some say that the movie *Mean Girls* is like *Seinfeld* for young women. The phrases, "Boo, you whore," and "Too gay to function," and "Gretchen, I'm sorry I laughed at you that time you got diarrhea at Barnes & Noble," conjure comprehension among young women the way the Seinfeld phrases "Soup Nazi," and "Not that there's anything wrong with that!" and "Believe it or not, George is not at home . . ." resonate with their parents. This is largely because society is obsessed with the idea of women—especially Supergirls—taking one another other out (and also because *Mean Girls* is a great movie).

Whether it is the depiction of "devil" female bosses tormenting their staffers in chick lit, sorority sisters raking at one anothers' arms while wrestling in inflatable pools filled with baby oil or

Jell-O, or beauty pageant contestants holding hands and baring their unnaturally white smiles wishing for their "girlfriends" to only be a runner-up, we love the idea of women pitted against one another. And, unfortunately, it is Supergirls largely supplying the truth behind this cultural phenomenon. When overachieving women attempt to measure their self-worth (clearly, a nonquantifiable thing), often their only means of measurement is comparing who they are better than and who they have to beat. Unfortunately, this fuels a toxic culture of competing for awards, seducing others' boyfriends, and being so hung up on outdoing other Supergirls that we don't have to time to realize that we are only making this nagging sense of underachievement worse for everyone as we play up the most to the standards that have made womanhood more like jujitsu.

Pegah, Age 15, Valley Stream North High school

Looking down the halls of Pegah's high school, one thing jumps out of the scene pretty evidently. It's a typical high school: muted colors on the walls and the lockers, bathrooms with frosted-glass windows, lots of noise, and lots of kids. There are some kids in really baggy jeans, a few in all-black ensembles, and a few in funkier outfits . . . but for the most part, a lot of the kids look the same. Sure, there is a lot of ethnic and presumably socioeconomic diversity—lots of varying skin tones and even some interesting accents—but most of the kids are wearing the same clothes and carrying themselves the same way. Especially among the girls, who pretty much all seem to be in tight jeans and nice hoodies or short skirts and sheer shirts and polos. They look sweet and nice (as girls are supposed to look), but often they're secretly warring.

"Girls can be pretty mean," Pegah says while shrugging over

a cappuccino at Starbucks on Sunday evening. Even among Pegah's closest friends, who mostly operate in a clique of ten girls, there is some cat fighting. While I'm hesitant to use and perpetuate the phrase "cat fighting" given that it's most often used to marginalize women's actual anger, the things that Pegah's friends seem to lock antlers about are a little ridiculous.

"There are just a few girls within my group of friends who don't like each other," Pegah explains. "They don't really know why; actually, I don't know that anyone does. . . . Most of the time, they try to be friends, but at other times, they're fighting and saying things about each other behind their backs. It kind of gets in the way of us all being friends. . . .

"It gets hard sometimes. Like, sometimes you have to pick whose side you're going to be on for things and it kind of gets everyone in a weird mood. Personally, I try to stay out of it, but they're *my friends*. I want things to be good with them and I think it's kind of silly that girls will turn on their friends when there's bigger stuff to deal with."

So does Pegah get in on this cat fighting?

"I do my best to stay out of it," she says somewhat elusively.

What's a relief for Pegah is that academically she doesn't have to be cutthroat with her friends (or worse, worry about them being cutthroat with her). As one of Pegah's friends put it to me during school, "Pegah is completely in her own league. There would be no point in trying to compete with her or, like, even try to get close to the things she does in school and the grades she gets. She's just *so smart*! Plus, like, none of us are in all the same classes as her because she's in all AP and accelerated stuff." (And, lucky for Pegah, her friends clearly hold her in high esteem and admire her, which makes the female infighting a little easier to bear.) But if she was competing with them for A's and the top test scores in her AP classes, it could get ugly.

What is a problem for Pegah is the boy situation. According to Pegah's clique, their one friend Chrissy is the one who gets all the attention from guys. Whether they're at school or at the mall, if someone is being approached by guys, it's Chrissy. The hottest guys at school like her, even though she's also pretty committed to innocent dating at this point. And while you can't fault a girl for being pretty . . . well, you can hate her. "Although you really *can't* hate Chrissy, because she's also really nice to everyone and stuff," says Pegah.

What's interesting is that some of the boys at Pegah's school and in her classes are a little rambunctious: I sense that the male ideal in high school is no longer the too-cool-for-school, blasé type of guy, but the ideal is rather somewhat inherently a class clown who tries to joke with the teachers and the hall monitors and makes everyone laugh. There were tons of guys like this in my school, too—wanting to be buddy-buddy with everyone and make people laugh.

However, while guys are appreciated for being "cool" and "funny," girls get the most points for being "nice" and "pretty." And the girls feel competitive with one another about fulfilling their roles. They can be mean and resentful when they feel that they're being eclipsed by another girl. But you don't see guys doing this . . . trying to work out more, tell their jokes better and louder, or slather themselves in more Axe body spray to try to extract more attention and affection from society or the people in their lives. So why are girls being so catty?

On the most intricate level, it's because there can only be so many beautiful, lauded young women at once, and the roles for what young women can do to be loved, be appreciated, and get really noticed need to be expanded to include "funny," "interesting," and "good the way she is." There can only be so much "pretty" and "perfect" girls, but there's no such thing as an excess of funny, approachable guys.

On the simplest level, girls are being so catty because they get a lot of attention for it.

Competition

I am competitive. Excessively competitive. I don't like anyone who gets in my way, and if it comes down to it, I will try to move anyone in my way. I'm a nice person and I genuinely *like people* (I'll attribute it to my Christian upbringing), but I am threatened by those poised to outdo me. Especially women.

And apparently, I'm not alone.

"I think fellow Supergirls will have intense feelings of competition/jealousy, and even if the Supergirl genuinely likes and cares about a fellow Supergirl, she will probably wind up feeling the need to outperform her," says Michele, a Long Island–based Supergirl and college student who aspires to become an investment banker.

> "I think fellow Supergirls will have intense feelings of competition/ jealousy, and even if the Supergirl genuinely likes and cares about a fellow Supergirl, she will probably wind up feeling the need to outperform her."
>
> **—Michele, age 19**

Says Amber Madison, the author of *Hooking Up: A Girl's Guide to Sex and Sexuality,* who also attended Tufts, a school known for its overachievers: "My inclination is that these perfectionists all must have a real competitive drive. I think ultimately overachieving is about competition, because it's achieving more and more than those surrounding you."

Competition is everywhere in young women's lives. For privileged girls, it starts with the rat race to get into a competitive preschool, then into a good kindergarten and elementary school (at which point the competition to be skinniest probably starts), then into a good high school (where there is competition to have the most elite boyfriends, the nicest clothes, and the nicest body), and a good college, and onto a good job, and finally to a corner office (or to a husband with a nice apartment). More middle-class or poorer girls experience competition in slightly more subtle ways. At chi-chi private schools, it seems that virtually everyone is smart (or rich enough that being smart wouldn't make a difference), while for Supergirls at public schools there is a high premium put on being in accelerated classes from elementary school through high school, which definitely requires some competition. In public high schools, there is competition for everything from class rank to becoming valedictorian to becoming prom queen to just being noticed.

Rachel, a high school student from upstate New York, feels like the competition in her high school has mostly to do with people wanting to be noticed and not wanting to be perceived as "ordinary." She says, "Everyone wants to stand out. Average is the most boring thing there is. No one wants to go unnoticed. It's easy for people to get lost in the crowd even when they are remarkable because everyone today works so hard to be successful and noticeable that everyone has to step up what they're doing to get some recognition." Rachel thinks that Supergirls are generally rewarded for their behavior. "Schools—especially the teachers—pay the most attention to the perfect girl who's on eight sports teams and such. Sometimes, a kid getting arrested will get some attention, too, but in general, you have to work hard doing good things to get noticed. There's no time for kids doing special stuff but also making time for themselves, so there's sort of this message that if you want to be noticed, you have to really run yourself ragged to compete with what other people are doing."

For Rebecca, a high school freshman from Syracuse, New

York, the competition has to do with staying ahead of the curve in accelerated and AP classes. "Sometimes when finals or midterms come, especially for math and the foreign languages—because they are some of the only advanced courses—it gets really competitive. It's mostly because there are only twenty other kids in the class, and I feel really stressed out because I'm competing with people who are as good as me."

But what do you do when you go to an elite prep school where the kids in all the classes are really smart and competitive? Maya, a high school junior from Washington, D.C., sees a lot of horn locking and intimidating at her private high school revolving around earning good grades and getting into college . . . and it seems intrinsic to the students. "The competition isn't necessarily more prevalent between the genders—the competition doesn't extend to 'I want to be better than this boy.' It's more like everyone for themselves." Maya also said that people look down on students heading to public schools or students deciding to apply to less prestigious private schools, but sometimes students will try to scope out who is applying to the same really prestigious schools and try to convince them not to apply so that there are less applicants from their school trying to get into the same dream college. "I know from a lot of my friends who have gone through the college admissions process, people will try to convince you not to apply or go to certain places," Maya says. But isn't that kind of an antagonistic environment to grow up in? That's the thing: Supergirls and overachievers can be competitive even with their own friends. "It's a toxic peer culture," Maya says. "As much as you think you know about a person, you never know how. There always has been a competitive aspect [in friendships]."

In college, the competition can be just as bad. "I want to murder everyone here some days," confesses Sasha, a junior

> "There is also a cattiness among women of color, and while there's always an element of meanness among women, it can be really hard to make friends with women of color."
>
> —**Sasha, age 21**

at UC–Berkeley. "People here are so sneaky; there is so much competition. I feel like we should be pulling together to help each other given that we are all taking really hard classes, but instead everyone is fighting against each other. Instead of helping each other out and being a support network, they try to outshine each other. Sometimes the female students here make jokes about all the other women except them being dumb. There is also a cattiness among women of color, and while there's always an element of meanness among women, it can be really hard to make friends with women of color. Women really tend to hate on each other."

Cheating is also directly tied into this competition. The rates of cheating in school are getting totally out of hand. According to Education Testing Services, an educational advocacy organization, between 75 and 98 percent of high schoolers admit to having cheated. Only, it isn't about beating the system; it's about students beating one another. Students are so crazed by the pressure in the institutions that they're a part of that they've turned against one another. Mischa, who studied biology at Johns Hopkins University, saw a lot of not necessarily unethical but sad behavior. "It wasn't like students were ruining the results of each other's labs, but if you wanted to start a study group or if you asked someone for his or her notes, you know, she'd look at you like you were crazy. People were friendly, but they weren't big on helping each other." And it's this unfair behavior that could breed a generation of adults who wouldn't hesitate to make unethical decisions in a work environment if it meant making more money or sealing a deal.

Clearly, this competition, unfortunately, doesn't end: it's in graduate school and medical school, it's in the waiting rooms of offices where applicants interviewing for a job are seated in a tense row, and it's among crazed young women trying to outdo one another to finally become "good."

This competition is especially pervasive in the dating scene, and even more so when Supergirls are tossed into the batch. The phenomenon is fairly universal: a guy who is with his girlfriend or a guy who is clearly courting a girl . . . being approached by another woman who sees the presence of another woman as her cue to go nab him. Or, there could be a group of guys mingling with a larger group of women . . . and the women compete with one another more fiercely over the guys than two lions eyeing one antelope on the Discovery Channel. This isn't because there aren't enough guys in the world or because women and men don't congregate in the right places. It's because women, especially type-A women, have been taught to take one another *out* over guys. Not to mention, how many times have we heard the phrase "'X College' to bed, 'Y College' to wed"? Whether it's Smith and Mount Holyoke, Barnard and Columbia, or Harvard and Wellesley, women at dueling colleges have been trying to accuse their counterparts of being too slutty for generations.

Something that absolutely floored me when I was talking with Supergirls for this book is how many of them expressed to me, without being prompted at all, how they don't like other women. "I just don't like them," some told me. "I just get along better with guys. I think they're nicer, smarter, and I just prefer to be around them," others confessed. "Girls are complete bitches," another said nonchalantly. And the problem with this is that women's being nasty to one another is completely encouraged in our society. The populace is captivated by women being bitchy: *Mean Girls* was a blockbuster for a reason; *Elimidate* draws late-night television viewers for the same (but less) reason; and Jell-O wrestling is a fraternity party favorite for female students looking for a form of sordid validation.

Yet despite this outward competition, if girls aren't secretive about their overachieving and their desire for attention from being perfect, it's a big problem. The phrases "secret studier" and "secret exerciser" have recently risen to popularity from girls trying to be sly about their quests for good grades or fitness . . . because they have to! Girls get totally threatened and annoyed by others' public bids for perfection, and the girls who are outward about their work habits and Supergirl prowess are perceived as annoying. Says Raquelle, a 19-year-old from Long Island, "There was this girl in my school who was always shaking and crying and freaking out from trying to do everything, and she was the valedictorian and ended up going to Harvard . . . but she didn't have any friends because she was so annoying about trying to be so smart."

And it's because of this competition that Supergirls aren't always well liked. While this overbred-puppy-of-a-girl is more of a Supergirl-gone-wrong than a genuine Supergirl, Raquelle articulates a point that being so high-achieving can exclude girls from the high school social culture. Some oddball Supergirls do spice up the batch, like the crazed Tracy Flick from the 1999 movie *Election,* whose overachieving antics made her develop a very antagonistic relationship with her peers and one of her teachers.

Truthfully speaking,

> "As much as you think you know about a person, you never know how. There always has been a competitive aspect [in friendships]."
> **—Maya, age 17**

you can be sympathetic to some contempt toward these hyper-competitive Supergirls. They break the curves; they take the best jobs. And it's really obnoxious for the non-Supergirls to be living a healthy lifestyle—eating enough, resting enough, respecting others' boundaries—and seeing others being rewarded for abusing their bodies and harmfully pushing their limits.

And sometimes, Supergirls are just downright annoying: in the *New York Times* article about "amazing girls," the girls who the reporter follows are painted as Christ figures (a hyper-Christian girl tells her friend that she can't make it to a meeting because she's feeding the homeless on Boston Common: "I'll come when God's work is done") and come off as really pretentious, showing off their true religions, talking in AP classes about being about "to reach some kind of state of independence and peacefulness and enlightenment," and having parents who discuss how they never rebelled. And while I can imagine that you're on your best behavior when you have a *New York Times* reporter in your house, the girls come off as obnoxiously saintly.

And I'm a fellow Supergirl . . . imagine how frustrating these girls are for the normal achievers! "Most non-Supergirls probably just feel frustrated and/or annoyed because they don't know why their Supergirl friend can't 'be normal," says Michele, a college sophomore living in Manhattan.

But, rather than bitching about the Supergirl behind her back, wouldn't it be more effective—and more along the lines of "friend duty"—to talk to this Supergirl about what is going on in her life and what is making her overachieve?

Supergirls sometimes even want to take out their friends. I feel some of my greatest twinges of jealousy toward my two best friends: I'd be lying if I said I wasn't contemptuous of the fact that Hilary is the star of the class at Cornell and always has boyfriends, and that I don't feel twinges of jealously toward Tara for getting perfect grades and having such a grace and warmth about her. But I love them both and I value their friendship the way I value clean drinking water and my three memory foam mattress covers (necessity and luxury).

Not to mention, if I wasn't me, I probably wouldn't like me. In fact, if I ever encountered another young person my age writing a book and writing articles and saving up for an Upper East Side apartment, I would feel seriously threatened. So could Supergirls ameliorate their collective dislike of one another with mutual admiration instead?

Bitches and Frenemies

My friend and I had a huge fight last summer and I yelled. I *YELLED!* And it amazed me: I had no idea such a huge sound could come out of my body. I probably hadn't so violently yelled in ten years or so, not since I was young enough to be pitching tantrums at the grocery store. Our society doesn't condition young women to get angry.

The manifest hypocrisy of this situation is that although young women are taught that competing with one another and intimidating one another and being nasty for the sake of outdoing one another are empowering or even glamorous, young women really aren't encouraged to *express* their anger. Talking behind other girls' backs, publicly making out with a boy who a frenemy has a very public crush on, or passive-aggressively staying up all night to outdo a peer or a coworker on a project are predictable actions among young women. When angry, it's normal to say, "You bitch! You are such a whore!" and send an e-mail to a few people (or, everyone in your contacts) about what an evil slut she is and how she is ugly and desperately needs a nose job. Yet, personally, I can't yell at anyone without starting to cry before I've made my point, and every time I take someone to task for something stupid she did, I end up feeling endlessly guilty about articulating the obvious. "People—even my parents—say that I'm a brat or that I'm a bitch," says Taylor, a high school student from western New York. "But I think they just say that because I speak my mind."

Perhaps the reactions Taylor gets are because when a young woman is frustrated by a peer or a coworker's flakiness while working on a group project, it's normal for her to be silently fuming but to do her peer's work and circumvent the problem. It's not normal to sit down with her peer and say, "Listen, I'm upset and annoyed, and I think we have some issues that we need to discuss and resolve," or, more directly, "You dropped the ball and it cost us." If it was the appropriate environment, the slighted young woman could say, "You are *suuuuuch* a bitch!" but she probably wouldn't.

It's casually understood that powerful women often feel intimidated by their peers and occasionally try to keep them down. But isn't this more or less the opposite of what guys do? Many argue that men have created an informal network—the "old boys' club"—to keep one another in power and to collectively feed off of one another's successes, whereas women seem to be threatened by one another's success and want to keep the ball in their court. But what are women supposed to do with all their power? After all, haven't we learned that trying to do everything and control everything only crush us?

As discussed earlier in the career chapter, the word *bitch*, although only five letters, has countless implications. Although some women have tried to reclaim the word so that it's "empowering," young women know that the word *bitch* is essentially used to describe a female grappling with her infantile frustrations, which we understand as being possessed by high school girls, sorority sisters, and female coworkers on some kind of PMS-induced power trip.

The reality is that our society raises girls and women to be nice. And although I hate to admit it, my "neutral mouth" is naturally in a frown, and when I'm thinking or daydreaming (which is essentially what I do when not engaged in conversation), my eyes get really big, which makes me look really pissed off. And people—everyone from my friends to the barista in Starbucks to the homeless guy in Washington Square Park—are always telling me to "smile!" However, I could never picture someone instructing my hulking, 6'4", 215-pound best guy friend to "smile!" Our society wants young women to be the peacemakers, the placators, and the "cheerer up-ers" . . . so no wonder why young women feel uncomfortable expressing their anger!

Koren Zailackas wrote in *Smashed: Story of a Drunken Girlhood*: "By now, I've accepted that I'm meek. . . . While that meekness won't help me make friends or get dates, it is favorable in other ways. Adults seem to think it makes me more feminine, and often, a little more grown-up. Teachers praise me for my cooperation. The 'comments' portion of my report card always reads: 'courteous,' 'attentive,' and 'well-mannered.' But teachers treat the domineering girls differently. Girls like [my best friend], who sit with the boys or speak out of turn, are called 'disruptive,' or 'disrespectful,' sometimes 'cocksure,' but even that sounds dirty."

"I'm not really surprised that the girls here are cautious about coming off as powerful, because look at really powerful women like Hillary Clinton: she's called a bitch all the time," says Chicago Hinsdale High School teacher Jared Friebel.

Similarly, look at Anna Wintour, the editor-in-chief of *Vogue* magazine. I don't doubt that she may be difficult to work for, I highly disagree with her body image politics, and I have absolutely no tolerance for corporate structures that treat their newer employees and assistants like crap, but Anna Wintour has done amazing things for the concept of women in business. When books and movies like *The Devil Wears Prada* challenge tough female bosses, isn't that a slap in the face to women's leadership skills? When David Carr set out to write an article for the *New York Times* in July 2006 about how realistic the portrayal of Anna Wintour in *The Devil Wears Prada* movie was, her friends—most notably Oscar de la Renta, S. I. Newhouse Jr., and the editor of the *New Yorker*—defined her more as a visionary. "She does not put a finger in the wind to judge trends: she is the wind," Carr wrote. "That is not to say that Ms. Wintour is anything approaching warm and cuddly—while she can be exceedingly droll and funny, she wears her impatience as others might wear a brooch. But that same characteristic in a male executive would seem not really worth mentioning."

This lack of respect for powerful women in the workplace doesn't give Supergirls much to look forward to. After all, what is the point of working your tail off to get into the offices of *Vogue* if your assistants write off your impatience as Satan in silk and get millions of dollars for it?

But what if a gal doesn't write a tell-all about the "bitch" she is in close contact with? What if she doesn't say a word? What if they pretend to be good friends, despite the mutual dislike? They're frenemies.

"A lot of girls say they don't like me," says Gina, a Supergirl sophomore in high school from Long Island. "And I don't know why it is, but all of my friends tell me that it's just because they think I'm 'too perfect.' Like, I don't think I'm perfect—I *know* I'm not perfect, but all of these girls say they think I try too hard to

> "Young women are encouraged to not voice their need to be noticed . . . what's problematic is that we don't recognize people doing positive things."
> **—Jennifer, age 25**

do everything and always be better than the other girls and. make it look like I'm not trying . . . or something," she says, trailing off and laughing. "It's totally stupid. But they pretend to be my friend anyway."

The concept of frenemies is pretty universal in the media: some of the most loved television shows and some of the beloved fictional media characters actively portray this really sad, misogynistic behavior. It was shown on *Mean Girls,* where Lindsay Lohan's character purposely gives Rachel McAdams's character foot cream for her face and "weight-loss bars" that make the Queen Bee balloon. In the books and on the TV show *Gossip Girl,* Blair and Serena are two Supergirl best friends—pretty, smart, popular—who really resent each other; in fact, they take calculated steps to sabotage each other, as Serena sleeps with Blair's boyfriend, and Blair makes it a point to ruin Serena socially. But they always end up making up! On *Sex and the City,* in one episode, Samantha befriends a woman who is just like her—loud, hypersexual, aggressive—who Samantha likes, but also grows to hate, mostly because of their similarities.

And perhaps that's exactly the problem! Because the female ideal today—being a well-rounded, sweet, pretty Supergirl—has every girls under the age of 25 comporting herself the same way, are frenemies rooted in the fact that girls are threatened by their virtual carbon copies? But it's heartbreaking: in the face of a perfection epidemic that threatens the well-being of virtually all girls in the United States, the most logical solution they see is to turn against one another! If girls feel that there is only so much love and attention to bestow upon the Supergirls, then it's every gal for herself.

Attention

In 2006, *Seventeen* magazine ran a quiz called "Are You Addicted to Attention?" which helped girls gauge if they relied too heavily on being noticed by causing fights, squealing, and acting outlandishly to make a scene; the story was accompanied by pictures of the Regina George character from *Mean Girls*, Lindsay Lohan yelling, and Paris Hilton flashing her typical flirty smirk. No offense to *Seventeen*, but it's this inaccurate portrayal of needing attention that is causing some major problems among young women.

Our society has taught young women that it is much easier to get attention for doing negative things. You can cause a nationwide media scandal in a day if you are a cheerleader and you post pictures on Myspace of you and your teammates in uniform posing with condoms in a store (like the cheerleaders of Texas's McKinney North High School in 2006) or if you distribute a video of yourself servicing a Swiffer mop (like the "HoMann ho" of New York's Horace Mann School who made a video of herself doing said activity in 2005). Being a smart girl doesn't cause a stir in quite the same way.

Unfortunately, the adults dominating the discussions on teens and attention don't have young people's best interests in mind. In fact, instead of seeing Supergirls' craving for attention as a red flag that society needs to recognize young women differently, some psychologists pin today's young women as cocky and full of themselves. Adult critics love to take on Facebook and Myspace as examples of teens being "narcissistic." "The world of online social networking is practically homogeneous in one other sense, however diverse it might first appear: Its users are committed to self-exposure," wrote Christine Rosen in the *New Atlantis,* a "journal of technology and society."

Despite dubbing herself a "member" of Generation Y, Jean Twenge, author of *Generation Me* and *The Narcissism Epidemic,* absolutely rips our generation in her work. In fact, in her books and various articles and interviews, she blames schools for teaching kids self-esteem, blames young people's sense of individuality, and rips Myspace and Facebook a new one. She told the Associated Press in February 2006, "We need to stop endlessly repeating 'You're special' and having children repeat that back. . . . By its very name, Myspace encourages attention-seeking, as does YouTube."

Ouch!

And while she may be right—these are attention-seeking gestures and there are countless young people who post information about their lives on Facebook, YouTube, Flickr, and their blogs as though they were famous—the question should not be *why are kids so full of themselves?*—but *why are young people so desperate for such a bizarre form of recognition?* What have today's young people—namely today's girls—been so deprived of that they resort to filling out silly surveys about themselves on their Myspace pages and uploading pictures of themselves on Flickr and Facebook making crooked pouts and holding up their rum and Cokes? While Twenge and her peers at San Francisco State see young people essentially saying, "Notice me!" as selfishness and a character flaw, I think it gives much zest to the argument that society doesn't notice the positive things that young women do and that girls must resort to body shots to gain recognition . . . despite that these are often the girls who are striving to get perfect grades and be class president.

"Young women are encouraged to not voice their need to be noticed, so it comes out in very different ways," says Jennifer, a graduate student studying sociology at UC–Berkeley. "The reason why people like Lindsay Lohan do the things they do to get recognized is because that's what they get attention for. Our society is very big on negative attention. . . . Look at a newspaper. . . . It's all bad news and failing government programs, but there are so many amazing people out there doing amazing things! What's problematic is that we don't recognize people doing positive things."

The activities that boys do also gain them more recognition: people don't come out in droves to see girls lead mock trial teams, but the guys' lacrosse games draw crowds (and groupies) akin to the NBA. Girls may never get comparable attention, but when they seek it, they often have to resort to more sordid measures.

Sasha, a junior at UC–Berkeley, sees a lot of her female peers acting as caricatures of themselves when they go out and when they go to parties . . . and for all the wrong reasons. "People confuse attention with respect. If a girl looks a certain way, people subsequently treat her in a way that's in line with how she looks, and people think the girl is getting some kind of compliment. Unfortunately, most girls don't have the strength or maturity to understand that the kind of attention they will receive is not a compliment or indicative of any kind of respect." But girls feed off of it . . . and I would really be inclined to argue that because girls haven't been raised with positive images of femininity and haven't been given appropriate recognition for their more substantive qualities, being hit on by guys or getting guys to look at them after dancing on a table at a bar is the closest replacement for respect and positive reinforcement for their accomplishments. Unfortunately this ideal of a drunk girl teetering on her stilettos on top of a bar sticky with spilled Sex on the Beaches only perpetuates a culture where women don't garner acknowledgment for being themselves. As comedian Mike Dugan wrote of pornography in his 2005 book *Men Fake Foreplay . . . and Other Lies That Are True*, it "becomes the only thing that will fill the emptiness that it creates."

Think about it: Paris Hilton got two months' worth of TV airtime in June and July 2007 for going to jail . . . but did anyone know that in those same months Emma Watson (star of *Harry Potter*) told *Parade* magazine about her belief in feminism, model and "then first niece" Lauren Bush diligently promoted her line of "FEED bag" purses that donate much of their $60 cost to the UN's campaign to fight child hunger in third-world countries, and Katie Roiphe got a job as the head of the journalism department at NYU? Discussion of Emma Watson's feminism was limited to the feminist blogosphere, Lauren Bush only got tiny mentions in *Vanity Fair* and *Time*, and, wait—who is Katie Roiphe?

(Roiphe, one of my favorite authors, published her first book—a controversial polemic about the date rape "crisis" on college campuses—when she was only in her early 20s.)

This all comes back to the uneven relationship between negative and positive attention: if young women want positive attention, they have to do so much more—they have to do *everything!*—to be recognized. But young women wouldn't have to rely on attention if they were able to feel good about themselves and know who they are and appreciate who they are. This is a huge part of why there is such competition today to get into colleges, to get jobs, to get fellowships and even boyfriends! When young women spend so much time perfecting themselves and trying to outdo one another, the standards become higher, and girls have to do more to get into college or win a scholarship or simply *be perfect* . . . but *they started* this cycle!

Here's the problem. If there is a girl who applies for and wins national scholarships, works insanely hard for a 4.0 and has various other successes as a movie extra or a venture capitalist, and wants *everyone* to know about it, many Supergirls' first instinct is *I have to outdo her.* However, rather than being contemptuous of this attention-happy Supergirl, shouldn't we feel sorry for her?

But there is good news in this Supergirl saga. These flashy shows of competition seem to fade with age. When I had brunch in October with Yolanda and her two good friends from middle school, there was no "frenemy" kind of vibe; what I saw was Yolanda and her friends being sustained and bonded by their friendship . . . not taking one another out in their interactions. If they were all bankers, nonprofit gurus, or hospitality managers, this would probably be a completely different story and a different kind of competition . . . which invites further delving into the concept of women in like industries being pitted against one another rather than forming the networks that the old boys do to collectively keep one another in power. But because they have their individual talents and prowess in separate industries, they could freely discuss work, vent about work, and also keep work completely separate from their relationships.

Completely in line with stereotypes of the New York banking world, there is competition at Yolanda's job. There's some envy over new accounts, some horn-locking to get those accounts, and an occasional sense of rivalry that's present in every office. "It's not really like people fight over stuff or whatever . . . we're an office, we're a team . . . we have to learn to work together. There is the occasional tension when someone outdoes someone else, but for the sake of appearances, they keep it to themselves." A little office rivalry in one of Manhattan's hottest banks is inevitable . . . where competition in young women's lives is the most interesting when its between friends and peers. If this kind of flashy girl-versus-girl competition is limited to younger cohorts, perhaps the pitting of women against one another is an expression of the insecurity that younger Generation Y-ers feel.

Although I have a few more socially acceptable years where I could get away with being a big bitch, I've tried to stop competing with and getting jealous of other women. I needed to reevaluate what happiness was to me and what true success was. The happiest moments of my life are not getting awards or article publications—things that are essentially mine at the expense of others. If I had to sum up the most important moments of my life in a quick flash of time, my mind would first go to sliding down a big yellow slide at Disney World as a child, going on a vacation to Paris with my mom and sister in middle school, losing my virginity on a freezing November night, watching *Superbad* with my sister and laughing so hard I cried, and having birthdays in Saratoga with my best friends. These are things that can't be competed for. And if someone else does see awards, promotions, and fellowships as her main source of joy . . . she should have them and be proud of them, and I hope she gets better one day.

chapter eight

"So, Do You Have a Boyfriend?"

Supergirls Should Be Sexy . . . and Always Have a Guy

He smelled like beer and deodorant and sweat, which is to say that to me, he smelled great—and I thought, Oh my God, it's really Cross. . . . Because I lived nine months a year on a campus of brick buildings and wooded hills and lovingly mown athletic fields, [his smell] conjured for me summer dances at country clubs, lives with wonderful secrets.
—Curtis Sittenfeld, from her 2006 novel, *Prep*

While many journalists and experts who have written about the lives of overachieving girls have argued that ambitious young women don't have time for boyfriends, just the opposite is true. Despite their superhuman immunity to fatigue, Supergirls are girls, too, after all. However, the stereotypes about Supergirls being too busy for boyfriends possess some aspects of truth: many Supergirls enjoy time-saving hookups as a form of manic sexual activity, a half-hour flash of physical intimacy that helps them "feel human again." Also, in a generation that was raised by the "faux empowerment" of raunch culture, well, sugar and spice just got a little bit spicier.

Today's Supergirls have to shoulder the pressure to be sexual animals yet still have to abide by the age-old standards of "purity." In fact, what it means to be "good" when it comes to sex is a contradictory message: we're told that virginity is embarrassing and that oral sex is the new handshake, yet old-fashioned sexism still teaches us that we aren't entitled to our sexuality.

Leah, Age 18, the State University of New York at Albany

SUNY–Albany is a sexy campus. Despite that within the grounds of UAlbany some of the most innovative research on nanotechnology is being brought forth by some of the nation's foremost smartypants, by the time Thursday rolls around, the focus is not on how to shrink things but on how to make the night larger than life. Because Thursday is the new Friday (Thirsty Thursday, anyone?), and drinking on most college campuses is condoned by the student body pretty much every day of the week with the exception of Monday and Tuesday . . . well, hard-partying students have a lot of drinking options. Virtually the entire nightlife scene in Albany is centered around SUNY students: bars in the "student ghetto" of downtown Albany only require student IDs from bar patrons, and even the more elite bar and club scene near the Albany waterfront has lenient admission policies, where knowing someone, having a decent fake ID, or being dressed provocatively can probably get someone in, according to students. Leah has noticed that police officers in the area won't even stop the slovenly drunken students crunching leaves on the sidewalks with beers in their hands, who either cracked open a beer on the walk home from the deli or left a dive bar with their unfinished drink.

Once, when Leah and her friends were walking downtown, visibly a bit intoxicated (and visibly underage), a police officer standing on the corner said to them, "You girls should be careful . . . there are a lot of really ugly guys out there tonight!"

Obviously, not only is the campus sexual culture conspicuous on the community level, but it's also viewed somewhat glibly . . . by some. The campus has an annual sexuality week with events and panels that seem to have the intention to both inform and be fun. In 2006, the programming included some slightly raunchy events such as "Sexual Jeopardy," "Loveline: Sex Talk at UAlbany," and "Nice Jewish Girls Gone Bad." However, in 2007, the programming became more cautionary, featuring workshops focusing mostly on rape, sexually transmitted diseases, and sexual health . . . and I wouldn't be hesitant to speculate that the more reserved content perhaps rooted from a very public rape on the UAlbany campus of a female student by two football players, and the rise of public discussion on the negative nature of today's college students' sexual habits.

In a generation that has been deprived of sex-positive, comprehensive, factually accurate sex education and communication about sex, drinking and sex go hand-in-hand. This is partly because alcohol is required to loosen the tension regarding sexuality, but also because in a hypersexual media culture, the teen sexual relationships we see on TV and in the movies geared toward teens preach sexual flashiness much more than showing how to be coupled, young, and in love. (Nick and Jessica were the exception, but we all know how that turned out.) MTV programming, *The Search for the Next Pussycat Doll,* and raunchy hip-hop songs reinforce to young women that the best way to snag a guy isn't by holding out for relationships but by being single and showing off their bodies. While Landon and Jamie of *A Walk to Remember* and Corey and Topanga of *Boy Meets World* (Oh my God . . . I just totally aged myself by referencing Ben Savage as a staple of my media-fed youth) were sweet, their monogamous youth romances were viewed as major anomalies . . . the kinds of things that could only happen on a select few TV shows. Hookups and casual sex are instead part of the sexual norm on college campuses.

"It's funny, on Saturday mornings, you see so many kids walking across the quads doing the walk of shame . . . but I don't see a lot of kids dating," says Leah. "There are some that do . . . they're the girls that are always with their boyfriends, just obsessed with them . . . and my suitemate, she's in a long-distance relationships, and that occupies a lot of her free time . . . but that's not your average student. People don't pursue relationships or sex like that."

When we meet up with Leah's friend Julia, a petite, loud freshman in a tight puffy coat, to go to a meeting, the girls talk about the night's upcoming student senate party: "The thing that sucks," says Julia, "is that I have a gynecologist appointment tomorrow morning, so I need to make sure that I don't do anything silly tonight." In addition to being too much information (and the inherent strangeness that she'd say this in front of a journalist, even though we were the same age), the inherent casual approach to sex is remarkable.

For now, Leah is enjoying being single. She just got to college and wants to keep her options open. She's not out to get a boyfriend—in fact, she has nearly ruled that option out completely, in part because of the aforementioned reason: no one dates!

However, I wonder to what extent Leah's constant working

plays in her feelings (or, rather, lack thereof) on her romantic relationships (or, again, lack thereof). Leah is so busy that she can't find an extra hour in each day to go to the gym or join the crew team (which she really wants to join!), let alone have a guy in her life. But I have a feeling that this is sort of a "chicken or the egg" situation. Does she not have a boyfriend because she's busy, or is she busy because she doesn't have a boyfriend?

Perhaps girls who aren't coupled and don't feel like they could be coupled (or have a steady stream of sex partners) overachieve in an effort to compensate or get that kind of validation. I will be the first to assert that trying to live up to the same sexual standards of your friends and community while living outside of that community's set standards of sexual attractiveness (read: being overweight) definitely complicates participating in the hookup culture . . . and I wonder if Leah's overachieving is a bit of a defense.

However, in a society that teaches girls that "being boned" (obviously, not my words) is the ultimate form of validation, don't honors like being elected a student senator or winning a $1,000-per-year scholarship for college (Leah won the extremely competitive New York Lottery Scholarship) pale by comparison? The honor bestowed in being a sexual conquest completely skews girls' value.

It's totally unfair.

Leah did hook up "all throughout high school. That was my thing," she says. "At parties and stuff, that's pretty much all I would do. . . . I'm taking it slow here, but eventually I might get back into it. . . . I don't know that it harms us, per se, but hookups are definitely a less intimate kind of relationship."

Despite having your face in a stranger's crotch. And therein lies the paradox.

Katie, Age 17, Syracuse University's School Press Institute

Those who believe a "boy crisis" exists could certainly find evidence of the phenomenon at the School Press Institute at Syracuse University.

"Holy sh-t," one of the boys at SPI says as he looks around the group of students at the campus tour that opens the first day of programs. "There are only seven guys here." Those seven guys immediately form a tight group and walk together in a bumbling clump as the pack of new students walk around the antique campus under the summer sun. The boys are mostly in either the photography class or the writing class, which means that the writing class has two boys. Both boys are shy in class, speaking quietly, and only speaking when they are called upon. Both are interested in sports writing, a competitive and male-dominated sector of journalism. When the students work in pairs, the girls who work with the boys do most of the work and the talking, and the boys nod and add the occasional anecdote. When they present their work, the girls, again, do most of the talking.

When Katie and her friends, and virtually all of the guys at SPI, go out to dinner at a Greek restaurant on Syracuse's popular Marshall Street, several of the boys don't seem to know how to conduct themselves at a restaurant: one lays down with his Walkman on and dozes off with his head on his backpack in the booth against the wall meant to seat people at the other bordering tables, two other boys speak three voice levels too loudly for a relatively nice restaurant, and the final two boys who attend somewhat rough high schools downstate loudly try to explain gang lingo to me and Katie's friend.

"It's like, 'Five down, six up,'" one of the boys explains to us, gesturing some kind of gang symbol with his hands. "It means that the Crips killed someone, so, now, like, the Crips are up. Like, they won."

"You actually have gangs in your school?" Katie's friend asks.

"Of course," says the other boy, as though students at every school put their gang terminology to use.

(Although it's interesting that he says this, because when I tried to independently confirm what "Five down, six up" meant, the closest I found to "six up" implicating illicit activity is that someone will yell "six up" when there are police coming to bust vendors selling drugs and beer at Phish concerts. So, either the gangs at this high school use underground terminology or there is a bizarre push for boys to model a knock-off version of gang life.)

At night, the kids retreat to the lounge in the dorms to sit and talk in the heat into the early hours of the morning, playing cards, charades, and "never have I ever."

The next morning when the girls wake up around seven to shower and have breakfast, despite that they are surely exhausted from having been awake all night, they feign cheerful "Good mornings!" to others walking in the dorm hallway and do their eyeliner in the bathrooms; they leave the dorms early to get coffee before class to get there on time. Their male counterparts, although standing upright and walking and giving nods of recognition to their friends as an exhausted greeting, don't seem to wake up until noon.

On the last day at camp, at the awards ceremony to recognize those who had been awarded scholarships and who had exerted extra effort at camp, the girls own. They are the majority of the scholarship winners and they take home virtually every award. And they earned it. During class, they sat up straight, listened, and feverishly took notes. During breaks, they scattered around Syracuse interviewing locals, store owners, and university officials for the stories that they were working on. They traded their rough drafts with their friends and scrawled edits and notes all over the papers.

On some level, camp really was a microcosm of a newspaper newsroom. The night before their stories were due, I had several girls ask me to look over their work, and, despite a few comma splices, I saw work fitting of college students and writers years older than them. Katie clocked hours and hours working on her feature story on Supreme Court Chief Justice John Roberts coming to Syracuse University to dedicate a new communications building; she tracked down Syracuse University officials, interest group leaders, leaders of campus and local political groups, and everyone in between for quotes and revised and combed through the story over and over again looking for the slightest issues to tweak. By the time she handed her story in to her teacher, it was nearly flawless. None of the boys asked me to proofread, and I didn't see them working on their stories together.

However, there is more to it than what meets the eye. On the first day of camp, when the girls noticed the extreme ratio to which they outnumbered the boys, they were a bit surprised:

"Omigod, there are, like, no guys here!"

"Are any of them cute?"

"Um . . . sorta?"

Within moments, the seven guys found themselves surrounded by girls wanting to know their names and where they were from and where they got their cool iPod cases.

It is no surprise that within a day, the pack of seven guys who stuck together in social situations melded with Katie's group of girlfriends, who, frankly speaking, were the prettiest, most popular clique of girls at camp.

At lunch, whenever a boy was speaking, the others gave him their full attention and listened and laughed wholeheartedly. The girls even giggled, and often there were more "ums" and "likes" inserted into their sentences. When it was just girls at a meal sitting together, they either errantly listened to one another and picked at their food or constantly interrupted one another with more interesting stories to tell. In class, when a boy talked, everyone listened and laughed passionately at his semi-funny jokes.

Although Katie wasn't really participating in this adulation (she had a boyfriend whom she called a few times throughout the week), it was clear that some of the boys had a real interest in her . . . although the girls' efforts to court the boys were much more pronounced.

In the end, the girls absolutely loved SPI. One of the girls described the camp to me as "one of the best weeks of my life." Journalism and making friends were the #1 and #2 focuses of the camp, respectively, but the girls also seemed to spend a lot of time trying to woo the guys. What's more surprising, however, is that few of the girls found the SPI boys to be particularly attractive or charismatic. "They're all at that weird stage in puberty where their arms are too long for their bodies," one of the girls laughed. "Some of them are kind of, like, *weird*," said another. "Like, last night, one of the guys was talking to me in this weird robotic voice for no reason and wouldn't stop. It's just like, *You're so awkward!*" So, why were the girls reverently showering the boys with attention and craving their attention in return?

Because despite that girls are encouraged to be smart and be leaders, there is still almost nothing more important to girls than getting approval from boys.

The Need for a Boyfriend

The stereotypical Supergirl tends to have a few things: a commitment to academics or work and all the trimmings (participation in leadership opportunities, extracurriculars, extra projects at work), style and savvy, a desire to please, and an endless goal of enticing the opposite sex.

The media coverage on Supergirls has argued that high-achieving young women don't need boyfriends. Laura Sessions Stepp pinpointed this as a cause of the college hookup culture in her book *Unhooked: How Young Women Pursue Sex, Delay Love, and Lose at Both;* Sara Rimer had a portion of her article in the *New York Times* about "amazing girls" under the subcategory "Who Needs a Boyfriend?" discussing how these girls were somewhat uninterested in male attention (although according to the girls' quotes, it appeared they were indeed very interested); and Dan Kindlon completely wiped out the concept of girls wanting to be coupled in his book *Alpha Girls: Understanding the New American Girl and How She Is Changing the World.*

Their arguments are true, but I would argue in a limited sense: having a boyfriend might be out among college students (wanting a boyfriend is still very much a yearning ache among high schoolers), but needing a steady stream of hookups or other romantic encounters is very much a part of how young women appraise themselves. A surprising number of the college women I talked to still define "hooking up" as the ultimate form of personal validation—and they funnel an enormous amount of energy into pondering, acquiring, and maintaining any sort of attention from guys.

In a little experiment, I decided that I wasn't going to gush to friends about my dating life and would not express much interest in hearing about theirs; lunch dates with my closest of friends became quiet and terse within a week or so. I have friends who will skip studying to talk on the phone to a boyfriend who goes to a different school or who will bail on a girls' night in a moment's notice for booty calls in another borough.

This pressure to be coupled is also evident in the way that the families and friends of Supergirls interact with them. At family or social gatherings, guys tend to be asked about their interests, their favorite sports team, their studies, or their work. The girls in the mix always deal with aunts, cousins, and family friends nagging:

"So, do you have a boyfriend?"

It used to drive me crazy at my parents' dinner parties that people always asked about my sister's boyfriends, but if they turned their focus on me and I explained that I wasn't seeing anyone particularly special, that would basically be the end of the attention I got (until I got a book deal, in which the question shifted to "How is the book coming along?" which could give zest to the argument that perhaps single Supergirls compensate for their relationship status with work).

However, I don't blame anyone, because even today, we still feel that a girl is only as good as the guy who will date her. Which, for Supergirls with near-perfect grades and big scholarships, is endlessly frustrating, both at the lack of appreciation for their undertakings and for the fact that they have to take on an even bigger undertaking carrying even more weight: finding a man. It's especially hard when our culture is just a teensy-weensy bit scared of powerful women.

Maureen Dowd, my personal idol and the only female *New York Times* opinion columnist, wrote in her 2005 book, *Are Men Necessary?: When Genders Collide,* that men are turned off by successful, powerful women. She attributed her single status to her high position at the *Times* and her position at the *Times* to her single status. In the quirky book *Privilege: Harvard and the Education of the Ruling Class,* Ross Douthat discusses that in his time at Harvard, women telling guys that they went to the esteemed school was called "dropping the H-bomb" and was really risky for the potential of a relationship. In an episode of *Sex and the City,* Miranda Hobbes pretends to be a flight attendant to get dates, because her actual job as a partner in a prestigious law firm was getting in the way of keeping guys around. So are guys turned off by successful, powerful Supergirls?

Yes. And no.

Like the movies *Maid in Manhattan* and *Pretty Woman,* there is a trend in making heroines out of women with low-status jobs who are highly undereducated and powerless by the standards of the men who covet them.

In a July 8, 2007, article, Hilary Duff told the London newspaper the *Guardian,* "It's hard for me to meet someone. I don't need someone who, like, has as much [money] as me, but I don't want someone who has much less because then you never really feel taken care of. And it would always make a guy feel not like a man." While there is so much to be said for Duff's sexism (in the same article, she says that she could never be a feminist because she doesn't want to date other women . . . as though acting in advocacy for women's rights automatically makes you a lesbian), she says more about guys and Supergirls. Are guys really afraid of a woman who makes that much money or is more "successful"?

> "Think about all the pressures that are on young women: we have to go to school, we have to be pretty, *we have to get laid,* we have to work, we have to graduate and then deal with our student debt, we have to get real jobs, we have to get married."
> —**Raquelle, age 19**

Being coupled is prioritized everywhere for girls. Look at teen magazines (and the 'tween magazines geared toward girls as young as 9): in every issue, the articles teased on the cover detail how to make a crush like you, how to seduce lifeguards and other cute guys you see who are at their jobs, how to be a better girlfriend, and so on . . . and yet there are only occasional articles on how to find the best college or why girls today are so sad.

It's not like this for everyone, though. "When I was in high school, while all my friends were freaking out about being single or working so hard to get boyfriends, I really wasn't," says Kayla C., a recent Wellesley graduate who works in politics. "And this was mostly my parents' doing. My dad was like, 'Why would you want to waste your time on some high school relationship when you are such a smart young woman and have all these wonderful things you could be accomplishing?' And I think that really rubbed off on me. I mean, I don't think I saw too much importance in being coupled all the time, and I did end up achieving a lot before I went on to Wellesley."

Being a "Good" Girl

Something that I found interesting was that while many of the Supergirls I interviewed for this book candidly—perhaps too candidly—told me about their eating disorders and how much they essentially hated their lives, many girls described sex in dodgy, circuitous terms. I personally understand the lingering stigma of talking about sex, but for girls who were so open about telling me about everything else, there was definitely a disconnect when they wouldn't say *vagina* or use the phrase *hooking up* as the authoritative verb to describe sex acts. It is, perhaps, one of the most honest portrayals of what we tell young women is acceptable behavior: have sex and please others with your sexual prowess, but feel and act as though you're very ashamed of it.

There is a definite imbalance in how Supergirls are taught to approach sex. Our society still understands young women to be sexual gatekeepers; intimidating fathers lecture their daughters' boyfriends on behaving themselves (or, at the very least, shoot them glares that would make even the most macho guy want to keep his pants on)—in fact, a summer 2007 T-Mobile commercial marketed the new Fave-5 plan around this very concept of a scary dad intimidating a girl's boyfriend because they were both in her Fave 5. It's understood that, in a dating scenario, young men would naturally want to be "wild" or "reckless," and young women should want to abstain—literally—given that they have a reputation to protect.

Says Gina, a sophomore Supergirl in high school on Long Island: "You want to look hot, and it's good to go out with guys, but personally, I'm not ready to, like, hook up, and I think at my age, like 14 or 15, it would be really looked down upon for a girl to be hooking up. Because, like, why would she be doing that?" Says Heather Corinna, the founder of the sex ed Web site Scareleteen.com: "The earliest ideas that we have about sex are usually the ones that stick, and, unfortunately, young women are being reared with the concept that they don't actually crave sex . . . that sexual desire isn't intrinsic to them; it's something men give them. . . . It makes girls very passive in their own sexual responses."

Meanwhile, ads all over the women's media

> "I think at my age, like 14 or 15, it would be really looked down upon for a girl to be hooking up. Because, like, why would she be doing that?"
>
> —Gina, age 15

are the polar opposite on the scale of teaching girls that they are genuinely powerful and that their sexuality is for them. They show girls that intelligence comes second to titillating and being genuine comes second to glamour. For example, the entire concept of Victoria's Secret commercials—that run during shows geared exclusively to teenagers—is to teach young women that to be sexy, loved, and complete, they need to be an extension of the Victoria's Secret brand, wearing VS lingerie and sacrificing their own power to make pouty faces and act as objects for guys' arousal.

This is where the tug-of-war comes into play, because today's young women have also been taught that their sexuality is currency and that they can use their bodies to gain acceptance. "Overachieving girls want to live up to what others think is perfect, but that formula doesn't work when it comes to sex, because what people think is perfect will differ," says Amber Madison, author of *Hooking Up: A Girl's Guide to Sex and Sexuality.* "So, some girls will get hung up on the virgin thing . . . but for others, sexually perfect is a girl who can have sex even if the guy doesn't care about her, because then she always wins and is never vulnerable, and she is still pleasing everyone. I think a lot of the time, no one is listening to what's going on inside; they're acting in a defensive way to try and score the most points with the different groups they are trying to please."

So, what happens when a Supergirl is at a party and the captain of the basketball team wants to hook up? Does the desire to stay "pure" for society trump the desire of a cute guy who really, really wants a blowjob? Whatever choice she makes, this is where the guilt ensues.

Guilt is a common reoccurrence in Supergirls' lives; young women feel guilty for eating a piece of cake, they feel guilty for sleeping until 11 on a Saturday morning; and they feel guilty for being sexual. This guilt gets to the point where many young women feel as though they are no longer "good" while participating in hookups or having sex; correspondingly, being sexual is labeled "bad." And what is so painful (and painfully ironic) about this sexual bind is that often young women aren't getting *anything* out of it. "Guys in their teens aren't good in bed at all. Getting worked up feels good, but I don't think anyone expects, like, orgasms or anything," says Rachel, a teen from upstate New York. I spoke with a high school Supergirl from Long Island who told me that there was some controversy in her clique of 15-year-olds, because one of their friends—a pretty blonde girl who worked hard to look sexy—had gone down on her boyfriend, and the girls didn't know how they felt about their friend getting so hot and heavy so soon. "Did he go down on her?" I asked out of mere curiosity. "Why would she want him to do that? That's gross and weird," she said with a touch of disgust in her voice.

> "Guys in their teens aren't good in bed at all. Getting worked up feels good, but I don't think anyone expects, like, orgasms or anything."
> —**Rachel, age 16**

"Women have this idea of, 'I need to look really sexual,' but society frowns upon the idea of women really being sexual," says Amber Madison.

Kira Cochrane wrote about this disconnect in a column for the *Guardian*, focusing specifically on how the Miss America pageant perpetuates this humanly unattainable balance of having to look sexy but being discouraged from wanting or pursuing sex (with respect to the 2006 Tara Conner controversy, when the reigning Miss USA was in trouble with pageant headquarters for not looking the part while getting drunk in bars and making out with other women, namely, Miss Teen USA).

There have always been beauty-queen scandals, of course—back in 1957, for instance, Miss USA, Leona Gage, was dethroned after it turned out that she was on her second marriage and had two children. But there have never been so many furores [sic] in such a short space of time and what they seem to prove is that beauty pageants—an anachronism for many decades now—are being crushed by their own internal contradiction, that the women involved should look sexually available at all times, but never actually be sexually active. . . .

. . . What also made [women] angry, though, were those long-standing rules that women must be chaste, unmarried and without children. Who was making these rules?

I am not a fan of beauty pageants, not only because they are *soooo* 1950s, but also because of how they dictate what makes a woman "good." And if you are looking at the sexual standards that beauty pageants set for young women, good is often equated with, as Kira Cochrane put it, looking sexual but not being sexually active. Says Rachel, a high school student from New York: "There is definitely this attitude that perfect girls can't be sexual. Teachers would probably be shocked to hear that their perfect student who sits in the front row and politely raises her hand to answer a question has sex or likes sex. But it's expected for a girl who is in normal classes and doesn't seem all too successful to want and need sex. Which isn't to say that girls who are over-achievers can't have healthy sex lives. . . . But then there is also this expectation [from their peers] for these perfect girls to be a 'Facebook girl,' to be one of the sort of careless girls who will put pictures of her and her friends getting drunk and posing in a sexy way, maybe humping each other, on Facebook."

The good/bad dichotomy is everywhere in the media—

especially the DIY media, like Facebook—with regard to sex. The pop singer Rihanna's 2007 CD was titled *Good Girl Gone Bad* to reflect the previously squeaky clean 19-year-old's transition from cheery tunes to sultry hip-hop videos in leather outfits. Two thousand seven was the year of the "bad girls," and the media circled around them, alternating between adulating them and warning of the influence they may have on teens; every publication from *Forbes* to *GQ* to *Newsweek* wrote about the "girls gone bad." "We've moved away from an obsession with bad boys to a fascination with bad girls with *Girls Gone Wild* and these out-of-control female celebrities," says Garance Franke-Ruta, the online politics editor of the *Washington Post,* who weighed in on the phenomenon in a May 2007 op-ed in the *Wall Street Journal* about how participating in *Girls Gone Wild* damages young women's reputations. "However, the 'bad girl' obsession is a very different creature: when we loved bad boys, there wasn't this massive cultural interest in them naked." But for the bad girls, that's really all it's about! While some of the "bad girls" drive drunk and almost drop their babies, the majority of the celebrity "bad girls" do nothing but flaunt their bodies (Rihanna's album cover for *Good Girl Gone Bad* is a picture of her posed with her hip jutting so that her butt makes up 80 percent of the picture).

One writer argues that the girls really trying to be good are the conservative ones. Writer Wendy Shalit published her second book, *Girls Gone Mild: Young Women Reclaim Self-Respect and Find It's Not Bad to Be Good,* in June 2007, discussing how young women have grown tired of the Pussycat Dolls and lingerie models pretending to represent femininity (and even feminism!), but this isn't a feminist book: Shalit encourages young women to return to traditional gender roles when it comes to sex. Shalit defines "good" as girls suppressing their sexual desires, and she reports that the girls who have found that it's "not bad to be good" are the ones who are okay with abstinence-only sex education in high school (the sex ed classes that define sex as solely for married people . . . end of discussion), who wear "modest" clothing by Christian fashion lines, don't have sex, and bake pies. The book *actually* includes a recipe for pie.

"Not only are there problems with this book in terms of the anti-feminism," says Erin Matson, an activist in the feminist group the National Organization for Women, "but I simply don't see girls participating in that 'trend.' At all."

Such discourse and discussion over young women's sexuality could be identified as one of the main reasons that so many Supergirls have such conflicting and often negative experiences with sex! Because we don't have a solid understanding of what is appropriate sexual behavior for young women and because there is so much guilt-tripping for girls who don't know how to answer to the various sexual demands made of them, there is nothing Supergirls can do to have "perfect" sexuality . . . and they feel like they can't ever be *good* in bed.

Raunch Culture and Sex to Fill a Void

I read Ariel Levy's book *Female Chauvinist Pigs: Women and the Rise of Raunch Culture* the summer before my sophomore year of college, and it was a total wake-up call for me. Levy discusses how, when young women see sexual power as peeling off their clothes for *Girls Gone Wild* videos or giving lots and lots of oral sex (without expecting anything in return), it isn't really empowerment. Levy argues that today's young women have been taught to embrace their oppression and cheerily participate in it to find "power," especially in terms of sex (it's quite fascinating: Levy draws parallels to *Uncle Tom's Cabin,* which depicts a slave who loves his masters, because his masters reward eager submission). What I got out of the book is that while mounting the stripper pole installed in the living room of a frat house[1] might *feel* like power, or seducing lots of guys might *feel* good, it feels good because the guys want to see women in a submissive, less cogent state, and guys reward women for fulfilling this un-2007 fantasy . . . but it's not power! Ariel Levy took a lot of criticism for questioning how we think about women's sexuality, but she essentially started the discussion revolving around raunch culture.

This raunch culture has definitely had it reverberations: the little girls I used to babysit for would run around the house yelling "Spring break!" and pulling up their shirts; everything can have sexual undertones; and it's remarkably not awkward when my mom and I watch *Sex and the City* reruns together. More broadly, however, I would argue that raunch culture has single-handedly fueled the hookup culture across the country. Despite the conservative constraints and pressures on them to be "good," Supergirls are eager participants in the hookup culture . . . because hooking up makes them feel *good* (both literally and figuratively).

Laura Sessions Stepp, a staff writer at the *Washington Post,* took on a thorough research project to investigate young women's participation in the hookup culture. In February 2007, Laura Sessions Stepp shocked the populace with her book *Unhooked: How Young Women Pursue Sex, Delay Love, and Lose at Both,* discussing the secret sex lives of the ambitious young women

---

1   According to a September 2007 article in the *Philadelphia Inquirer,* many fraternities, most notably at Arizona State and NYU, have installed stripper poles in their frat houses.

she met at GW and Duke. Sessions Stepp discussed how these incredibly intelligent young women traveled alone across campus during the middle of the night for booty calls, got insanely drunk and danced on top of tables, and used sex to (try to) gain power or social status. Needless to say, her findings were macabre and shocked the media.

Something that shocked me during the first year I lived in the dorms for college was how the young women around me—who, for the most part, were white, affluent, intelligent young women who chose Pace's honors program over admission to NYU or Fordham—didn't seem to suffer from eating disorders or disordered eating at the rates that I expected. Despite being the kind of young women who you would except to have eating disorders, they drank sugary cocktails voraciously and ordered greasy Chinese food at midnight, and there was surprisingly little post-meal purging. They did, however, have the craziest approaches to sex. There was a ton of hooking up going on; people approached sex in a manic fashion, engaging in intercourse five or more times in one retreat to the bedroom or with more than one partner in a night. One-night stands completely lost the "taboo factor"; in fact, going home with some random guy was fodder to brag about in the dorm lounge on lazy Sunday evenings. During these chats, girls revealed to participating in some sex acts that I don't think even the writers of *Sex and the City* would be so brazen as to discuss.

People were bringing strangers from the neighborhood bars back to the dorms so often that the building's security director called a mandatory assembly in the school theater with the hundreds of residents in the dorm to discuss why it is not safe to drunkenly sign strangers into the building. Unfortunately, his speech kind of lost its punch when he said in this thick Italian-Brooklyn accent, "I don't want to have to call your mom and say, '*So, yo' little Suzy went missin'. So we stah-ted an inves-tigation . . . and we found her und-ah the bridge. You know why? Because she made an a-ass outta ha-self. And now she's dead.*'" Needless to say, the "audience" had completely erupted in laugh-ter before he could really get into why it was bad to have sex with strangers. So, when they weren't hosting, girls would ride the subway far into Brooklyn or take the train from Penn Station into New Jersey at all hours of the night for booty calls, regardless of whether they had to be at work at 8 in the morning or if they had a test at 10.

So what were they doing? Seeking validation and trying to be "good," the same way they did with helping a professor with pro bono research or folding an extra load of laundry for their mom. Except when a guy shows a Supergirl that she's good enough to be laid, it seems to mean more than making the dean's list or getting a promotion at work—because, as discussed earlier, male approval seems to be the ultimate form of validation among these hyperambitious young women. And while these girls—several of them my good friends—will argue with me that these booty calls are empowering, at the simplest level, the words that our society uses to describe heterosexual sexual activity among young peo-ple—being screwed, being boned, getting "done"—irrevocably take the power from young women and make "hookups" about women being dominated.

It takes many young women—myself included—some time to stop thinking of their sexuality as currency, as something that they could offer up in trade for validation . . . however, it doesn't take that long to realize that the feeling of being "good" from hookups lasts as long as the average guy's orgasm. Without sounding like a 1950s throwback, I feel like sex within relation-ships—even if they're new relationships—is the way to go.

It's not all macabre sexual rituals, though. In fact, when

Supergirls can pursue romantic relationships that are about treating one another as equals, that romance can really help them get through the struggles of adolescence, the ups and downs of college, and the occasionally turbulent 20s.

And perhaps the hooking-up trends aren't what they seem. Says Amber Madison: "There is this trend of girls saying, 'I can't have a relationship because I don't want one,' when in reality that's a defensive thing, because girls have been told by so many people that guys don't want relationships, that they want sex." The problem is that sometimes the guys are under that same influence, where they've been raised to believe that *they* only want sex, when in reality they don't always want to have the endless anonymous sex that their female counterparts are willing to offer. So—wait for it—some guys really do want to have pad thai and pinot grigio on a Friday night and watch movies at home. Well, as long as Mom and Dad aren't home, in case things do heat up.

chapter nine

"My Mom's My Best Friend"

Supergirls Will Make Our Parents Proud . . . at Any Cost

"'What have I always said is the most important thing?'
'Family.'
'I was gonna say breakfast . . . '"
—Jason Bateman and Michael Cera as Michael and George-Michael
Bluth in the cult-hit TV show *Arrested Development*

They say that young people who go to Hollywood crave the attention celebrities garner because they weren't loved enough as children. So what does that mean for kids who crave the attention inherent in mentions in the local newspaper for earning awards, scoring the final soccer goal, making valedictorian speeches, leading fund-raising events, graduating Phi Beta Kappa, and so on? Very little. The families who breed Supergirls are as varied as the Supergirls themselves. However, there are families who reinforce every stereotype about the overbearing parents manufacturing "perfect" daughters, as there are the sexist families who made it clear to their daughters that they had something to prove, as there are the happy families who have no idea why (or really, *how*) their daughters are balancing such overbooked appointment calendars . . . the latter of whom seem to make up 80 percent of the parents of Supergirls. Psychologists argue that, in general, parents want what is best for their children, and that seems to be apparent when it comes to Super girls. What families need to do, in light of the shifting "American dream" complicating family life, is band together and keep lines of communication open about love, life, and gender roles and be more vocal about how proud they are of their daughters.

Pegah, Age 15, Valley Stream North High School

During the time that I spend with Pegah, she is grounded for what, to an outsider, seems like a negligible offense. "My parents had a guest over for dinner the other night and I was really hungry, and I asked my mom what time we were having dinner. I guess I said it in a kind of whiny tone, because after their friend left, my mom was like, 'You can't embarrass us like that in front of a guest! You can't go out with your friends after school on Friday!' and then my dad pipes in like, 'She can't go out all weekend!' So here we are," Pegah says, motioning around her kitchen. She has set up camp at her desk in the all-white kitchen, where her books, folders, and stack of flash cards are pristinely organized. Even though she's at home, she still looks great with her hair up and in beige yoga pants and a pink velour hoodie, although she doesn't really looked relaxed.

Her home is beautiful. True to the archetypes of the modern Long Island home, the house has wall-to-wall white carpeting, black leather couches, a nice television, and modern-looking dining room furniture. The entire house is pristinely clean; if it weren't for the photos of Pegah and her older brothers framed around the living room, it would be fair to wonder if people actually lived here. The house is wired; they have five computers, two of them laptops, and the phone rings every hour or so. They live in a neighborhood about five minutes away from Pegah's school; the houses on their block all have groomed lawns and decorations like pumpkins and autumn-themed flags outside for the fall. Their house is one of the bigger ones on their block, and with newly painted shutters and siding, it's probably the nicest looking, too.

Pegah has a lot of pressure on her; she clocks longer hours studying and working on school stuff than your average adult professional does in any given week at work. Some fingers could be pointed at her parents, but when I meet them the next morning, there are fingers pointing everywhere.

Pegah's father is a soft-spoken, stern man, probably in his mid-50s. He is a math professor at a local university. On a Saturday morning, he is home from work and wearing a suit around the house. Pegah's mother is an incredibly well-mannered woman who works at the perfume counter in a department store in the upscale Roosevelt Field Mall in Garden City, New York. ("It's the best job ever for discounts," Pegah says.)

"We want to give her whatever we can that we can afford," Pegah's dad says. "We want her to have a nice Sweet 16, we want her to go to a very good college, we want her to have the richest life possible. And we want her to go out with her friends and be happy. . . . We just want her to be mindful of success, too. . . . She is a kind, sweet, caring girl. My only concern is that she is very sensitive to the idea of what her friends think of her."

"How am I sensitive to what my friends think?" Pegah asks.

"She cares very much about how the house looks when she has friends over," her father says directly to me. "She always wants to be the best; she becomes uncomfortable when there are others above her."

"But how does that make me sensitive?" Pegah asks, slightly irritated.

"It's just that she really tries her best at everything, and when she doesn't exceed her own expectations, I think she becomes very upset," Pegah's mom says carefully.

"You can't act like I'm, like, this way on my own, though," Pegah says quickly. "I developed a lot of these behaviors from your encouragement."

"Yes," Pegah's dad says. "We very much encouraged her to be successful . . ."

" . . . and I sort of took it from there," Pegah says. "But you still do contribute to the way I act."

Pegah's dad admits, "We are a little more strict with her."

"A little more *careful*," Pegah's mom says, correcting him.

Pegah's dad nods. "We like that she goes out with her friends, but we always want to know where she's going, what the phone number of the house is, and that she'll be back early. And no boys—"

"I already told her about that—" Pegah says quickly. She had: when I gauged the topic of sex and hooking up the day before, Pegah told me that hooking up wasn't her style and that the word *dating* wasn't allowed to be said in her house. "I'm not allowed to date until I'm out of high school," Pegah had told me.

"Yes, no boys," her dad says and nods finally.

"We're more careful with her because she's our only girl," Pegah's mom says, "and she's our last. We take care of her and protect her differently." But Pegah isn't even allowed to go to sleepovers . . . isn't that a little extreme?

Pegah's brother gets a watered-down version of the expectations on Pegah. Pegah feels that he was encouraged to be just as successful, but because he didn't latch on to the concept, neither he nor his parents really pursued his overachieving.

Whereas when Pegah showed that she wanted to succeed, the bar became progressively higher. After all, whenever I hung out at Pegah's house, a steady stream of her brother's friends came and went, and the sound of video games (and boys yelling about video games) poured from his room at all times.

Pegah refers to her parents as Mommy and Daddy; she is very close with her mother, who tends to be a little more lenient and, for example, took Pegah shopping on Sunday when she was supposed to be grounded. Pegah's parents come off as incredibly strict—and highly protective—but they obviously want their daughter to be happy. Perhaps the gap between Pegah being an overachiever and having moderation is lost in translation from her parents being immigrants and her being a first-generation kid living in what, to her parents, is a completely different world.

"My parents try to teach me the difference between hobbies and careers. Lawyer—that's a career. Surgeon—that's a career. Interior designer, fashion designer, actress—hobbies. And teacher? That's not an option. But I really feel like I could be a teacher and be really happy. I don't care that much about the money. If I can take care of myself and contribute towards my family, I think I could be just as happy being a teacher, a seventh-grade teacher. But my parents want me to hold up this standard of being successful so I'll have money so my kids can have these same opportunities as I did."

"We came to this country working very hard, and we want our children to uphold that hard work," says Pegah's dad. "So, we want our daughter to be very successful, and while we also very much want her to be happy, if she was acting in a way or was pursuing a path that we didn't think was in line with our way of life, we would say something." *Yeah, so Pegah, about that teaching thing . . .*

But then again, Pegah's parents seem to seek moderation from their daughter: "During midterms and finals week, my dad pays me to stop studying. Like, this past spring during finals, my dad tried to take away my books and told me that he'd pay me to go do something else. But obviously, I took my books back and I didn't take his money. I just felt like I needed to do more and kept studying."

The Hothouse Daughters

One of the biggest questions that kept coming up in my research was this: Are Supergirls born or raised? Virtually all the Supergirls I met fell in or in between three categories: (1) their parents put little-to-no pressure on them, and they felt this push to "be everything" from society, the media, or other outside forces; (2) their parents encouraged them to excel, a message that was blown totally out of proportion by society's pressure on girls; or (3) their parents doled out insane pressure that essentially enslaved them.

I grew up with possibly the greatest caricature of extreme parenting since *The Overachievers*, where Alexandra Robbins told the story of a high school student being locked in her room by her mother, forced to study for the SAT. This girl who I grew up with was essentially born in a picket fence pressure cooker. From kindergarten through the tenth grade, Fifi's mom was *the* helicopter mom. According to rumors, Fifi's mom dyed her daughter's hair light blonde; this was actually kind of conspicuous, given the girl's straw-like hair and the jet-black roots that sprouted from her head for the second half of every month (what's perplexing is that it was okay for Fifi's brother to be a brunette).

By the time we were in elementary school, Fifi had perfect manners and perfect penmanship, and comported herself like a smiling doll that opened its eyes when it was in the upright position. By high school, Fifi was the president of every club she was involved in, played several sports, and dressed herself as though J. Crew had employed her to wear their nautical brunch-in-Nantucket-themed mannequin ensembles in public. She cried once when she got a 98 on a test, and in fact, Fifi cried fairly regularly in school and cited the pressure her parents put on her as the source. Plus, she drank so much coffee that I'm getting acid reflux just thinking about it. Now Fifi is, to the best of my knowledge, a pre-med major at one of the country's best colleges, with a schedule as tiresome as the one she possessed when we were 16—but she is driving herself.

It seems that these obsessive parents are most prevalent in privileged environments. Maya, a senior at the prestigious Washington, D.C., prep school, the Georgetown Day School, sees lots of her classmates being pressured by parents to be perfect. "The parents of the kids at my school are really successful people . . . a lot of *Washington Post* reporters, *Washington Post* columnists, diplomats, White House staffers. So there is a lot of pressure along the lines of, *My dad works at CNN, so I have to work somewhere good, which means I need to get into a good college, which means that I need to study hard right now.* And it's not like their parents told their kids that they have to be successful; usually, it's unspoken pressure."

However, Maya said the pressure isn't always this implicit: "Although a lot of kids simply see their parents' important jobs and understand that they are expected to re-create their success, a lot of parents do lay out the expectations for their kids." Especially their daughters—a girl in Maya's class was the paradigm of prestigious prep school students: her father was a Washington insider who went on to become a top administrator at a top university, and her mother was a stay-at-home mom who wanted nothing more than for her daughter to be smart, accomplished, and thin. The girl's mother put a lot of pressure on her to be perfect: the girl could only go out with her friends one night a weekend because she had to spend the rest of the time studying, she wasn't allowed to come to dinner if her homework wasn't finished, and she shouldered a lot of pressure from her mom to be

skinny . . . even though the she was 5'8" and 130 pounds, which nearly qualifies her as underweight. During a family camping trip, this mom pressured her daughter into doing a five-mile run in the morning, which the girl did, and in the afternoon, her mom insisted they go on a long hike. The girl was so exhausted during the hike that she ended up flipping a disk in her spine. "Her spine is permanently damaged and she can't exercise anymore because of it," Maya explained.

Says Allison, an upstate New York high schooler: "In my family, there is definite pressure to be perfect. I know my mom wants perfection from me. Most of the people in my family didn't finish college, so partly there's that vicarious pressure to go to college and be successful for the people in my family who couldn't. Also, my cousins are all around my age, more or less, and everyone my age is very bright, so it's kind of competitive within my family. I feel like, if I'm not doing something at all times, my family will be disappointed in me."

"I think my generation had a lot more free time and our activities were a lot more of our own initiative," says Garance Franke-Ruta, the online politics editor of the *Washington Post,* who grew up in the '80s. "Our parents had a slightly more laissez parenting style, sort of 'free to be you and me.' Today there is a different generation of parents; today's parenting is somewhat more intensive, and given that there are a lot more people in America now and people make a much bigger deal out of going to places like Harvard, I think parents are pushing for their kids to have greater competitive drives." (Franke-Ruta, who went to Harvard, doesn't consider herself an overachiever and seemed embarrassed by my fawning over her alma mater.)

She even explained that some refer to the Generation Y-ers as "teacup kids," in reference to the teeny-tiny overbred puppies that are always shaking and urinating in inappropriate places out of constant anxiety.

Some parents do take their overbearingness totally over the top. There are huge stereotypes that immigrant families and families of Asian and Middle Eastern descent put tremendous pressure on their kids and that their children turn out to be hyperstressed: while these stereotypes are racist, they are also mildly entertaining, and like most stereotypes, often true.

> "There is definitely a norm in the Iranian-American culture of having high-achieving children."
>
> **—Bahar, age 21**

"My family is Persian, from Iran, and it plays a huge role in how I always feel like I could always be better and how I have so many different roles to play," says Bahar, a college student from Texas. "I teach Farsi classes, so I feel like I have to be a *good girl* and be more conservative and appear very responsible, mature, studious, and even appear as a traditional Iranian woman in that context. There is definitely a norm in the Iranian-American culture of having high-achieving children. Parental social circles always compare their kids and are like, 'My daughter is an honors student and she got a scholarship to this school . . .' and there is definitely that pressure to achieve so your parents can say something good about you to their friends. Sometimes my parents and I will be talking about something that they want me to do, like a competition or a community service thing, and I'll be like, *Do you just want me to do this so you can tell your friends about it?* And obviously, I can't say no, because that would be letting them down."

And sometimes it gets *totally* out of control: Mischa, a researcher and graduate student in the biology department at Johns Hopkins University, almost always went with the wishes of her demanding parents. They expected her to do well in school and enter a lucrative field, so she graduated from the University of Toronto with a degree in biology and went on to Johns Hopkins.

"They always had high expectations, but I knew it was their way of showing their love." However, when Mischa got engaged to a guy at Johns Hopkins who was not of Indian descent like her, her traditional parents went ballistic.

Soon afterward, Mischa's parents called her with bad news: her grandfather in India was sick and dying, and she needed to come see him for the last time. So, she put aside her differences with her parents and flew to India to see her grandfather. However, one tiny problem arose: when she got there, her grandfather was totally fine. Her parents lured her there to get her away from her American fiancé and had no intention of letting her go back to the States. Unfortunately, she was greeted with some stark news when finally she got back home: "My parents informed me that they were disowning me for not respecting their wishes." Now in therapy dealing with posttraumatic stress disorder from being essentially kidnapped by her own parents, Mischa is gaining a better sense of self. To top it all off, she had an absolutely lovely wedding a year later, on her own terms, her way.

And sometimes well-intentioned parents don't mean to do the damage that they do. Often, it's purely a matter of environment and socialization, like it was for Morgan, a 20-something who grew up in a wealthy Colorado suburb: "I was raised in an upper-middle-class neighborhood in Colorado, and there was definitely this culture of having perfect children in the all-white suburbs. I don't think my parents ever outwardly pushed me to be the perfect child, but I think there was this expectation to uphold the upscale image that goes along with ballet classes, piano lessons, and horseback riding . . . the whole picket fence, 12-year-olds-with-cell-phones kind of thing. . . . I was always a busy child with my lessons, and I think I grew up understanding that I was supposed to always be busy."

Says Jennifer, a graduate student at UC–Berkeley: "We are all psychologically built differently, and some people have this obsessive personality as a tendency, but I think a lot of young women's perfectionist behaviors are really learned, especially from the family. For me personally, I knew my parents loved me unconditionally and that they just wanted me to try my hardest; they didn't care if I had an A or B in a class at school. . . . I think what it is for me is that my parents weren't home a lot when I was growing up; I was a real latchkey kid, so I wonder if I thought if they'd be home more often if I was just 'better,' and I think it just really accelerated into . . . this all-out mentality of having it all, being really nice, never getting angry, never getting stressed out, being pretty, arranging parties, and finding the perfect partner well before I turned 30."

And other times, what seems to be overbearing parenting is actually totally accidental. "I remember being a kid and coming home from school with a test that I got a 95 on, and my parents would be like, *Why didn't you get a 100?*" says Laura Jeanne Hammond, editor of *Next Step* magazine. "And while I totally knew they were joking and that they were very proud of me, on the other hand, them saying that did articulate the fact that I didn't get a 100 but that I probably could have."

The Other Side of the Story

When I asked the Supergirls I interviewed where they thought the pressure to be perfect came from, almost all of them said "the family and parents."

"Does your family or your parents put pressure on you?" I would ask.

"Oh, no!" most would say. "My mom is *sooo* cool," or, "No, I get along fine with my parents. It's just other kids' parents that put pressure on them."

In fact, I think the majority of parents of Supergirls are shocked at their children's behavior. "When I would stay up really late in high school studying and doing homework, my mom and dad were like, 'What are you doing? This is stupid. Go to bed!'" says Kayla, a recent Wellesley grad. Parents, in general, seem perplexed that their children, who they raised to have structure *and* fun, seem to be taking lifestyle pointers from Opus Dei members.

My best friend was *the* Supergirl in high school (had great grades, played on two sports teams, popular, woke up at ungodly hours to curl her hair before school, and got virtually no sleep but was still unusually nice), and her parents were completely bewildered by her austere and tireless behavior. In my house, there would be some major tension when my mom would come downstairs and see me at the computer in the middle of the night slaving over my AP American history homework. By the time my sister was a high school junior, my mom put her foot down. "This is insane. Go to bed. I will write your teacher a note saying that I said you aren't allowed to do this much homework," my mom would say. My mom would joke that she was the only parent who would ever vouch that the dog ate the homework . . . although I don't know that my sister ever took her up on the offer.

"Almost every family-themed movie you watch, there is so often this idiotic, sometimes slightly sinister mother figure who wants her daughter to be perfect and marry the perfect guy," says Dr. SuEllen Hampkins,

> "My parents were always really big proponents of an A-. My mom was always opposed to making me feel like I needed to be perfect."
> **—Emily, age 24**

a psychologist and author of the book *The Mother–Daughter Project*. "These characters evade the fact that the vast majority of mothers don't want their daughters to be perfect; they want their daughters to be happy and self-confident and not fall victim to these propagated ideas."

Conversely, I think that the real problem affecting today's parents and their children that may have played a part in cultivating Supergirls is that there aren't open lines of communication between parents and their children.

I don't think that young people feel like they can come to adults with their problems, because the things that Generation Y-ers—and especially Supergirls—are dealing with are often on territory that would downright *shock* adults if they knew what was going on. "I think each generation is considered a rebel to the generation before it," says Heather Corinna, the author of *S.E.X.*, "and while young people are pushing the boundaries on what their parents did, parents are always shocked, because what young people are up to surpasses what they did, but also because we don't want to recognize children's transformation into adulthood." Yet I feel like the things that we're doing are crass beyond what even the kids of the 1970s would joke about doing (although a trusted adult figure assures me that kids have been having sex in the back of Catholic church parking lots for decades, if not because of the pot they smoked, then just for the irony of it). And, I think that the pristine reputations that Supergirls work so hard to maintain prevent some of them from reaching out for help—even if they really need it. If a Supergirl is dealing with an Adderall problem or feeling miserable after a string of hookups that didn't provide the validation that they supposedly promised, it's really hard for her to go to an adult who thinks this Supergirl is the brainy girl next door only to find out she's been fooling around with the boy across the street.

In her 1994 book *Reviving Ophelia: Saving the Selves of Adolescent Girls,* Dr. Mary Pipher identifies an unfair double standard in development that demonizes moms: "Relationships with fathers are portrayed as productive and growth-oriented, while relationships with mothers are depicted as regressive and dependent. Fathers are praised for their involvement with children. Mothers, on the other hand, are criticized unless their involvement is precisely the right amount." While I would maintain that mothers' parenting styles are still put under the microscope, fathers who don't take an active interest in their daughters' lives have children who look to outside sources for validation.

The negative effect of lacking dads in young women's lives has been a recent mainstream media focus. I would argue that this started with John Mayer's song "Daughters" in 2005, where Mayer crooned about daddy issues. Then came Lindsay Lohan, who (probably accidentally) made public what goes wrong when you have a poor relationship with your father: at 17, Lohan was living with 23-year-old boyfriend Wilmer Valderrama and went on to spend her 21st birthday in rehab, with a prison sentence looming over her. Then came the father-issues-riddled Supergirl Meredith Grey on the television show *Grey's Anatomy,* who attempted to bed all of Seattle and stayed in an unhealthy relationship with her boyfriend (also her boss, "Dr. McDreamy"), purportedly because of her tumultuous relationship with her father.

Sexist family structures are hugely damaging to girls. In families where it is made clear to girls that being female isn't necessarily a good thing or that being female automatically chips away at a person's power, young women learn that they have to compensate for their gender by being extraordinary. If girls in high school see their moms, ten years younger and half as moneyed as their dads, cooking dinner for the family after a long day at work, what kind of message does that send?

Erika, the equestrian from New York, feels a sexist imbalance in her parents' pressure: "My younger brother is a really good soccer player. He does soccer camps, will play on summer soccer league team, and is a really strong runner. He definitely achieves, but he doesn't get pushed as hard as I do. When I don't do something right, my parents will take things or privileges away from me, but he doesn't deal with that. He has an 85 average, and our parents are like, 'Good job!' but when I was in his grade, I had a 95 and I didn't get any encouragement for that kind of mediocrity. And even though he has an 85, when I get an 89 on an occasional test, my parents are like, 'You have to do better.' So naturally I feel a little inadequate if my brother doesn't have to do half the things I do, but he's considered twice as good as me." So, what will it take for Erika to be good?

Says Jordan, a senior at the University of Arizona, "I've struggled with my body image and trying to be a certain way and I've always felt like there's less requirements made of guys . . . maybe it's penis envy. Having a younger brother, I see how much easier it is for him than for me. While my mom has always forced me to go to college and get good grades, it's always been easier for him. He's not always held to the same standards. He enrolled in community college, he didn't like it so he switched to part-time, and then he dropped out of school. It also has to do with me being a first child, maybe more so than me being a girl, but I've tried to avoid disappointing my mom."

Not to mention, the way our society speeds up youth means that the family doesn't sit in the family room after dinner with the kids watching TV and the parents reading *Life* magazine: with the academic pressures put on kids, adolescence—which could be a precious time of being a semi-adult and being able to gradually become friends with your parents—is riddled by hours of homework, chugging Red Bull at 10 at night while arguing with Mom about where a missing biology folder went, and college admissions anxiety galore. This anxiety is often transposed onto the family, when really it could be very much lessened by families banding together.

"Properly faced, adversity builds character," wrote Dr. Mary Pipher in *Reviving Ophelia*. And I think that this is key when examining the issues facing the "average" American family. There are such pressures on teens, such pressures on parents, and the blame gets thrown left and right while individual families may be about to implode.

Instead, there is something to be said for banding together. Fittingly, in Dr. SuEllen Hampkins and Renee Schultz's 2007 book, *The Mother–Daughter Project*, the pair of psychologists suggest that groups of mother–daughter pairs make it a point to meet and discuss the issues they face, to promote teamwork, bonding, and open communication. While I concede that it sounds awkward for young women, whose most structured talking with their moms happens in the car on the way to a meeting while munching on a cereal bar, I think that the occasionally antagonistic relationships that my friends and I had with our moms during adolescence could instead have been converted to powerful, intimate relationships and sources of strength. If I consider the lowest points in my life, the most trying times of struggle, the only person who was able to make it genuinely better was my mom. The mother–daughter bond is endlessly powerful, and if young women can sort out the miscommunications that they have with their moms about what is expected of them, it can be a really cathartic relationship.

Many sociologists argue that the United States practices familialism, where people are willing to sacrifice things and occasionally act against their own self-interest for the betterment of their families . . . and that's pretty cute. On a more basic level, the fertility industry wouldn't make $3 billion annually if couples didn't so desperately want to have kids. So what we need today is communication. Parents' actions, whether it's not paying enough attention to their kids or not giving their kids enough praise, are silent messages that can easily be construed as "you're not good enough," when really parents can get overwhelmed or can assume from media reports that their kids want 'space and don't want to be slathered with attention. Meanwhile, because of the constant media reports saying that praise is bad, perhaps parents are biting their tongues before saying, "Great job, I'm so proud of you!" when they want to say it but think it might be harmful. Perhaps teens need to explicitly say, "Notice me!" And because the media paints adolescence as this scary time where teens give themselves tattoos and are prone to "losing it," parents may be hesitant to ask teens how they are doing and what they're up to . . . but I was always really excited when my mom randomly said, "Hey, do you want to go to Starbucks?" or, "Hey, want to go to Stockbridge for the day?"

Even though society and the media instill young women with the belief that they could always be better, families can be the force that turns that sentiment around and teaches them that it's *good* to be a girl.

chapter ten

"I'm as Good as Any Guy . . . Right?"

Supergirls Believe in Equality . . . So Why Are We Afraid of the F-word *(Feminist)*?

....

> *Those who don't learn from history*
> *are doomed to repeat it.*
> —George Santayana

Today's girls are *busy.* They make sure that every hour of their day is accounted for, whether it's school or work, and then clubs and sports and volunteering and meetings. This is in addition to unscheduled although ever-present time spent fixating on their weight, their appearance, their relationships with guys, how others perceive them, and whether their pointer toes are freakishly longer than their big toes (and other worries that wouldn't actually be worries in a more normally functioning person). As such, there is something funky going on here: Although Supergirls complain about the vastness of their schoolwork and the pressure to be pretty, are they perhaps purposely overloading themselves with obligations and anxieties in an effort to distract themselves from something bigger? Are the Supergirls purposely signing up for eighteen college credits and an internship in an effort to avoid coming face-to-face with their problems?

While today's busy Supergirls spend more time looking forward than looking back, we might be surprised to realize that our mothers and grandmothers dealt with many of these same worries and concerns. In 1963, a feminist writer named Betty Friedan wrote a book called *The Feminine Mystique* that discussed how housewives had been feeling anxious, upset, and unfulfilled, but it wasn't appropriate for them to explore who they were and what they really wanted, so they joined book clubs, took on positions within the PTA, and made extravagant dinners, in an effort to distract themselves. It seems that women historically have overworked themselves and busied themselves in order to avoid confronting the situation. Luckily, there's a remedy for this: feminism.

Allie, Age 20, George Washington University

On an arbitrary Wednesday night in October, Allie and I sit in a restaurant/pub in Washington, D.C.'s young and largely student-populated Foggy Bottom neighborhood. The pub is known for their burgers; they make almost thirty variations of the American culinary staple, and the restaurant is packed full of kids in jeans and polos washing down quintessential pub fare with beers. Allie and I are out by ourselves, both young women in a big city; we're both relatively economically independent (or will be shortly), both studying women's studies in school, and both very cognizant of our place in the world. We're a tad entitled and totally game for whatever life throws at us. This is progress.

Allie has seen Dan Rather walking on the street, shaken hands with Katie Couric at a school event, and been hugged by Jimmy Carter after he gave a controversial speech at GW and she approached him at the ensuing reception, telling him that she liked him and that she, too, was from Georgia. Allie met all three of the 2008 Democratic primary front-runners: in fact, she once had a ten-minute conversation with Barack Obama and an amusing encounter with Hillary Clinton.

"She came to do an event at my school, and because I worked as the assistant to the university's master of events, I got to run around backstage and watch Hillary give a speech from the wing of the stage. . . . So Hillary kind of strode off the stage when she was done speaking and walked up to me and these other two kids from University Events, and she asked really sweetly—'Do any of you know where I could find a water bottle?'—*for the record, not 'Get me a water bottle!'*—and all of us just stared at her and blinked, and after five seconds—literally five seconds—of silence, I just piped up and was like, 'I don't know where there are water bottles, but I think you're amazing.' And she just smiled and laughed and was like, 'Oh, thank you!' And then I was like, 'Hi, I'm Allie,' and she was like, 'Hi, I'm Hillary.' And we shook hands and talked for a little while."

However, despite that Allie's career at GW is the picture of feminist progress—opportunities like this have never been open to young women in other ways her unrelenting schedule can be seen as a surprising throwback to earlier times. Read on.

Allie's days are insane; from 8 in the morning to 5 at night, she is out doing *something*—studying, interning, working, going to class—and she comes back to her apartment to cook dinner and maybe watch an episode of *The Office* or *Grey's Anatomy* before setting off to do more homework and prepare for the next day of scheduling insanity. She is involved in lots of clubs . . . particularly clubs that have nothing to do with her and seemingly play no role in her future, like directing high-pressure drama club plays and doing layout for GW's impressive (and demanding) student newspaper the *Hatchet*. Allie has made it abundantly clear that she does things that will get her from her position today as a student to her future career as a political lobbyist, so for someone who has virtually no free time, it's bizarre to see her devoting lots of time and energy to activities that seem to lack any part of the trajectory of her career goals.

The next night, Allie and I have dinner with her roommate at her (huge, absolutely gorgeous) apartment in Washington's endlessly hip Dupont Circle neighborhood. Allie cooks chicken and pasta with pesto for dinner while her roommate, a tall, pretty blonde from Indiana, works feverishly on her computer and then tells us about her long, crazy day leading school clubs and dealing with university bureaucracy. Allie's roommate seemingly busies herself all day, all the time, with various, mostly unrelated clubs and internships, even though she doesn't have a goal in mind. "I'm just on autopilot," she says of her schedule, running between jobs and internships and clubs. "This is what I do." End of story; she shrugs, cracking open a can of diet Coke. However, human beings don't naturally take on more obligations than they can handle and busy themselves to the point of exhaustion . . . just to keep their options open. Being this busy without a goal in sight—and perhaps without a substantive goal, like getting into medical school or getting off welfare—is actually kind of self-defeating and stupid.

There has to be something going that makes young women busy themselves all the time, even when they don't really know why they make their schedules so packed. Obviously, we've told young women that this is their role, to be completely overextended, all the time . . . but if they're exhausted and not happy with the various roles they play, doesn't this resemble a time before women's progress? In fact, doesn't this resemble when women were told that playing their prescribed roles as homemakers would make them happy . . . and it just didn't? The desperate housewives of the 1950s were supposed to find themselves in enjoying new appliances, sewing, and making homemade canapés . . . which is about as purposeful as trying to find yourself in taking eighteen credits of 300-level college courses.

I spent a few hours one morning in a Starbucks on the GW campus and was absolutely struck by the extent to which the female GW students looked like "trophy" students. There were girls in runway-caliber outfits sitting in the faux velour chairs at 9 in the morning, sipping designer coffee and brushing their purposefully straightened hair out of their faces. Only they were highlighting in and ferociously perusing their textbooks, copies of the *Washington Post* were scattered around the seating area, and students chattered manically about this meeting and that interview and those tests. But does anyone know why they're doing what they're doing? Are the Supergirls' manic work habits some kind of defense mechanism? Possibly. And if so, this isn't the first time this has happened.

This Isn't Actually Necessary

I recently went to a party with a friend where the host told us to "bring something." I stopped at the liquor store down the street from me and bought a bottle of wine, while my Supergirl friend spent an afternoon making and assembling a homemade cookie platter. However, my Supergirl friend is also a chronically overscheduled person who had a ton of work to catch up on that weekend . . . and she hates cooking. Needless to say, there is a big disconnect between girls' have-to's and girls' want-to's. The problem is that it seems girls are doing these tasks merely to fill up their time, not giving themselves a second to breathe; the Supergirls' overscheduledness seems quite intentional.

Raquelle recently graduated from high school on Long Island, New York, with a host of acceptance letters to good colleges and an impressive activities résumé, having participated in varsity sports and led school clubs for years. But she's not a Supergirl: she's happy and healthy and has plenty of time to hang out with her friends . . . yet she recognizes that if she wanted to bury herself in work, her leadership positions, sports commitments, and job could provide enough work to distract her.

"These things we do don't have to take that much work. . . . I think teachers and students design clubs so you can put in the minimum effort possible and still have them on your activities résumé; it's only these crazy girls who decide to make these clubs into a lot of work. If they wanted to, they could do what they had to do in ten seconds and not make a production out of every little thing. I think they're searching for some validation for their existence. Accomplishments, that's what they define themselves by . . . they don't have to search for what their personality is. They're not happy, satisfied people. We admire them because they make the schools look good. . . . Schools like that they have this person who has this 100 average and is this pillar of society. . . . But I think these girls' involvement isn't really a good thing."

Some of the things Supergirls do *don't* require as much effort as the Supergirls put into them. Supergirls really don't need to make homemade cranberry macadamia white chocolate chip cookies for donors to eat at the school blood drive; store-bought ones would suffice. There is no need spend three hours making handwritten posters for French club meetings; they could be typed on the computer, printed, and put up in five minutes.

There is no need to spend all night making special hair ribbons for the cheerleading team; there are three Redwood trees' worth of catalogs of cheerleading supplies for ordering things like that.

The deal is this: today's young women are really stressed and are missing something in life, but instead of coming face to face with the issue and letting themselves be alone with their thoughts, they overwork themselves and stay so busy that they can't confront their problems. The Supergirl syndrome (when taken to its extreme) is really a coping mechanism, a way of dealing with our own fears and insecurities. Instead of confronting how society has taught us that growing up female isn't a good thing and isn't fun, girls take to straightening their hair, making homemade posters for student elections, and giving everyone and their brother rides to school as a distraction.

Virtually all of the five Supergirls who I got up close and personal with did this to a certain extent. Leah spent a ton of time merely organizing, and while her days were admirably over-scheduled, I feel like her organizing and self-micromanaging had more in common with my habit of cleaning when I don't want to do something that I have to do, rather than actually needing to have her schedule written out in three different places every day. Given that when I visited her art history class, we watched some cracked-up movie in Chinese with these giant puppets in a cherry tree field and then her teacher lectured for eight million years about art and stuff, I feel like an A in the class would be achievable through pure B.S.-ing on the tests, let alone taking rigorous notes during each class and turning them into meticulous outlines like Leah did.

Pegah's weekend was completely consumed by her independent science research, but let's think on classic teen girl scale: Pegah had a stack of thirty-page medical journal articles to read and chose to carefully peruse each article, highlighting as she went along and going back to really try to comprehend the key bits. However, given that she has no intention of becoming an endocrinologist, at 15, there is no reason for her to need to so intricately understand hormonal imbalances in bipolar patients. Any teenage girl—even a good student—would probably take each article that Pegah had, find the main point, and make sure she was proficient enough in understanding the topic to have a quick conversation about it with her research mentor. Pegah's workload could have taken an hour or two . . . not an entire weekend. But if she *wanted* it to take an entire weekend, it totally could, and others could write it off as a mind-blowing work ethic rather than perhaps a distraction from the fact that she's being forced into the medical field at age 15. Ditto for Pegah's AP world history summer assignment: when Pegah handed in her nearly fifty-page summer assignment, her teacher wouldn't accept it because of how long it was! The assignment was probably intended to take a day or two, not an entire summer. But for Pegah, completing that assignment was probably a perfect distraction given that she had an entire unstructured summer to think . . . and would probably get to thinking about things that would challenge her way of life.

While I would argue that most Supergirls' self-distraction is to lure their thoughts away from broader issues of being raised with a latent understanding that it's not good to be a girl, sometimes Supergirls' work is meant to distract them from something more concrete. Christy, a Supergirl who was recently sexually assaulted while living in Missouri, can definitely identify some of her overachieving and overscheduling as a means to distract her from something very specific: "I think that my 'overbusyness' is a big result of just trying to cope and trying to feel numb to what's happened. I think that experience in particular kind of devalued me on some level, and I think sometimes all of my work and passions are driven through reaffirming my value in the world. It's like through my work I tell myself, 'I'm a good person, I contribute, I do fund-raising for nonprofits, I got a law passed in Missouri to help with the collection of forensic evidence for rape cases'. . . . I feel energetic and driven, but it's both a good thing and a bad thing."

There is an interesting asymmetry when you compare these young women's lives to young women who *had* to work. Jennifer, now a graduate student at UC–Berkeley, grew up in a rural town of one thousand in northern Texas, where working your fingers to the bone wasn't called overachieving—it was called making a living. "I grew up in this working-class background where I started busing tables at a restaurant when I was 10, and when I was 15, I started working forty- to fifty-hour weeks in the summer while also helping my mom clean houses; it's what we had to do to pay bills. The idea of working several jobs is just something that I've gotten used to, so balancing everything at school and at college was a natural progression."

Jennifer has absolutely no hostility toward her more privileged Supergirl peers who worked similar schedules doing very different tasks—baking gourmet cookies for school bake sales at 2 in the morning, spending entire afternoons at the gym in fruitless attempts to banish stubborn arm flab, and clocking forty hours a week studying in order to ace the SAT—and could have had the more laid-back adolescence that Jennifer was prevented from having because of economic necessity. Although Jennifer does recognize the incongruity that the Southern belles who she went on to meet at college had led similarly overworked adolescences, for completely superfluous reasons, she says, "I think human beings really need security, passion, and validation, and I think it's sad that more privileged girls can't relax and enjoy their time that they don't have to spend working . . . but I don't fault them at all."

Jennifer is a little more saintly than I am. I'm comfortable asserting at this point in my life that although I do go totally overboard with obsessing over the blondeness of my hair, the whiteness of my teeth, and worrying about pleasing people, the gross number of hours that I dedicate to sitting at my desk working is more income driven. I work as hard as I do for money, because I'm becoming an adult and need to pay for my own rent, food, and clothes. As such, I have *no tolerance* for my Supergirl friends who make their relatively light workload and two club activities for school into a sixty-hour-a-week obligation and then proceed to whine about it all the time. Not to mention, my friends are going above and beyond on research papers and group projects that their teachers often receive and think—like Pegah's teacher—*Why would you do this much? I don't want to have to read three drafts of this twenty-page research paper so that you can have the A you were going to get anyway.*

But it's not fair to dislike these girls for this. After all, society made them this way. They've been conditioned into this behavior, of working and working and working in order not to pay attention to their needs. Actually, they've been conditioned into a lot of things.

> "Feminists worked really hard to get us the privilege to take AP classes . . . it was them that made it cool to be smart."
>
> **—Erika, age 16**

A Role for Girls

Our society doesn't have a set role for girls and young women. Today's young women have been raised with incredibly convoluted and often contradictory messages about what it means to be female, starting as young as early girlhood. For the girls, there was *Baywatch* Barbie, Mermaid Barbie, and a host of Disney princess dolls, in addition to Doctor Barbie and Mulan (who kicked butt). Actually, Disney gave pretty clear-cut indications of what being female meant: Ariel in *The Little Mermaid* sprouts legs and goes to earth and attracts a prince despite that she has no voice and can't talk. Snow White stayed at home and cooked and cleaned while the seven dwarfs went, well, you know the song: *Hi-ho! Hi-ho! It's off to work we go!* Children's movies like *The Parent Trap, It Takes Two,* and *Au Pair* all show that a woman's role is to be a mean, beautiful maniac who marries a well-off man for his money, but doesn't have attributes outside of good looks and a sugary smile to hide all that scheming.

(I cannot believe the extent to which I just dated myself. To recap for those born after 1992 who probably didn't watch these movies as children, *It Takes Two* was an early Mary-Kate and Ashley Olsen movie where the twins are identical strangers who meet and try to keep one of the girl's millionaire fathers from marrying an evil young woman . . . which is pretty much the plot of *The Parent Trap,* except that Lindsay Lohan (and Lindsay Lohan) are actually sisters. In *Au Pair,* a made-for-TV ABC Family movie, two children have to try to stop their millionaire father from marrying a golddigger younger woman and help him fall in love with their nanny.)

In preschool and elementary school, all the teachers are referred to as *Miss* (or sometimes *Mrs.*); I didn't learn that *Ms.* was a word until the third grade when I tearfully argued with my mom about her choice to write "Ms. Funk" on her name tag when she chaperoned a class trip, unlike almost all the other moms who had written "Mrs.," which is inconceivable to me that so many mothers in 1997 would prefer to be identified by their marital status. It's unlikely that children see many men associated with their caretaking and education, which establishes a very unfortunate stereotype about which gender is in charge of child rearing and which gender wears suits and has business cards.

In high school, teachers discuss how historically women haven't been able to participate in the mainstream of society; in history classes, students learn that women are raped as a tool of battle during wartime and that women were not able to participate in the founding of the United States. In the context of today's garbled roles for women, students don't automatically assume *And this was not a good thing* and teachers don't articulate that. By junior and senior years, there are both spoken and unspoken expectations that young women lose their virginity, dress nicely, and achieve the stereotypical high school experience. More credit is given to the girls who are small, quiet, and who listen than to the girls who shamelessly say what they are thinking; more credit is given to the cheerleading squad captain, who leads in an ancillary role to the boys, than to the captain of the girls' basketball team, who leads in what is actually a complementary role to the boys' power.

But many of today's girls grew up with girl power. When I was in the third grade, five loud, scantily clad British women changed the landscape of gender roles in Generation Y: the Spice Girls, giving peace signs and yelling "GAHL POW-AH!" told girls that being female had some inherent power. While many argue that "girl power" was a marketing device designed to sell more CDs—and also corrupted the concept of feminism, given that the Spice Girls trudged around in eight-inch-high platform boots and miniskirts, spilling out of their tops—it was one of the first mainstream media campaigns that said "It's good to be a girl." *American Girl* magazine launched in 1992 as a magazine geared toward 8- to 12-year-old girls, teaching them about how to start their own summer business, how to feel beautiful on the inside and out, and how to become successful (every month they ran a profile of a "real" woman role model). On the children's television show *Rugrats,* one of the children's mothers was a business executive who brokered deals on her cell phone and had a male assistant; the set of twins in the cartoon had a mother who lifted weights. Although Abercrombie shirts that say "Who needs brains when you have these?" scrawled across the chest are available to girls, so are shirts that say, "One day, a woman will be president."

(Although, interestingly enough, this is a shirt that Wal-Mart executives pulled from their racks, claiming that the shirt's message undermined the store's "family values," which gives more zest to the argument that our society can't collectively make up its mind as to how young women should comport themselves.)

But when I was hanging out with Gina, a 16 year-old Supergirl in upper-middle-class Garden City on Long Island, I commented on the row of girls in miniskirts and tight Abercrombie T-shirts sitting on a bench watching the boys play baseball for fun after school at her former middle school.

"It's very 1950s, but that's still what girls do. The boys are the active ones, and the girls sit there and watch. And that's not what *all* girls do, but that's definitely how they get approval from the guys. I think the guys like knowing that the girls are there watching, the supporting role. It's so stupid, though!" But at the same time, this Supergirl had consistent near-perfect grades, was on three sports teams, and was poised to go away to a highly competitive college in two years, to study journalism. So how can these girls, in miniskirts and batting their eyelashes, exist in the same era let alone the same *school* as this Supergirl?

Hence, look at all these different roles! Girls are simultaneously taught that they are waiting to be rescued and that they are strong and powerful. It's a society where girls see strong, smart characters in books, such as Hermione Granger in *Harry Potter,* but in the promotional movie posters for the fifth movie, *Harry Potter and the Order of the Phoenix,* Emma Watson (the actress who plays Hermione) was Photoshopped to be thinner and bustier (although Daniel Radcliffe and Rupert Grint, the male actors, were left undoctored in the photo). Girls must sort through these different messages and figure out which combinations of conflicting traits will make them good and loved and accepted. "I envy the fact that boyhood's rules are consistent," Koren Zailackas wrote in *Smashed: Story of a Drunken Girlhood.* "Being male is not a mess of contradictions, the way being female is. It is not trying to resolve how to be both desirable and smart, soft and sturdy, emotional and capable."

I think much of this confusion is what breeds girls who bend over backward to please everyone. Today's young women have been raised with these completely impossible expectations . . . so when they are not able to fulfill all these competing roles, not only do they feel like disappointments, but they'll do whatever they can in their power to make up for their "inadequacies." And they're raised to thrive on bettering themselves—even if it comes at the expense of their physical, mental, or emotional health. They have no clue how they're supposed to act and what they're supposed to be doing, so they do everything and get a lot of positive reinforcement for compensating for their discomfort.

"And it's this being a *girl* that teaches you that nothing you do is good enough."

—Erin, age 26

The Problem Without a Name

Although we colloquially understand the 1960s to have been a time of flower power, unisex bell bottoms, and lots and lots of drugs, in many suburban reserved areas of the country, the 1960s much more closely resembled the 1950s than Woodstock. Most women were still having passive anticlimatic sex and ironing their husbands' shirts, rather than pursuing free love and making tie-dyed shirts. This was women's prescribed role, and they were supposed to enjoy it.

After five years of rigorous research, in 1963, Betty Friedan published *The Feminine Mystique,* in which she discussed how housewives who were doing everything they were supposed to do and keeping busy all the time—decorating a beautiful suburban home, keeping their husbands happy, raising five children, volunteering with the PTA, going to book clubs and fun classes, and maintaining their prim appearance—weren't actually happy. They were constantly doing something, yet they were miserable. They were so wrapped up in leading Campfire Girl meetings that they couldn't explore their situation. One woman told Friedan, "I thought I had to be there every afternoon when [my children] got home from school. I read all the books they were assigned so I could help them with their schoolwork." Friedan called them to seek something more in life: "A baked potato is not as big as the world, and vacuuming the living room floor—with or without makeup—is not work that takes enough thought or energy to challenge any woman's full capacity. . . . This is the real mystery: why did so many American women, with the ability and education to discover and create, go back home again, to look for 'something more' in housework and raising children?"

The Supergirl dilemma, on paper, is the exact opposite of the feminine mystique—today's young women have virtually no lack of opportunities. But theoretically it's the same oppression of women that today's Supergirls' grandmothers dealt with in the 1950s and 1960s: our sexist society is teaching young women to busy themselves from exploring the pain that our sexist society created! Similar to how the homemakers of the 1960s were supposed to find themselves in their perfect homes and their smiling children, today's young women are taught to find themselves in making flashcards and being student body president . . . but self-exploration can't be on someone else's terms.

After all, the Supergirl dilemma isn't new: it's just "the problem without a name" in a tighter outfit with more cleavage showing. Betty Friedan told women in her book, "It is easier to live through someone else than to become complete yourself." And while it doesn't seem to make much sense to apply this quote to the lives of Supergirls, if you look deeper, it makes so much sense! I would bet that if it were up to the majority of Supergirls, they would not be spending Saturday mornings at lacrosse practice or jogging before volunteering at a car wash, but sleeping late and reading *Cosmopolitan*. If our culture wasn't obsessed with where our friends and peers went to college, I'd wager that many Supergirls would pick a more laid-back college over the constant demands of Princeton or Columbia. While hard work is showcased on Supergirls' résumés and is credited to the Supergirls themselves, much of the time, the things that Supergirls do aren't for their own pleasure. They're just going on autopilot, keeping themselves as busy as possible in order to prevent some kind of emotional revolt against their roles . . . one thing they've been explicitly told wouldn't be acceptable.

In a world where girls are raised to believe that they aren't good enough the way they are or that they aren't good enough as girls—whether that's through boys being favored in school, emaciated girls setting standards of beauty on billboards, women being portrayed as functionally retarded on MTV—perhaps they believe that being leaders in clubs and having every second of their days accounted for will make them worthy of the air they breathe. And perhaps this exhaustive busyness keeps them from asking the important questions: *Why am I working so hard? What am I trying to compensate for? When am I going to feel good enough . . . and why don't I feel good enough now?*

Although young women today are juggling work, school, working out, volunteering, going out with friends, and keeping tabs on their families, some women still feel strangely unsatisfied as they collapse into bed after a long day.

Supergirls should try to figure out who they really are and what they are genuinely passionate about. But before they can try to change things, they have to recognize that the way things are going isn't good. Our society needs to acknowledge that there is still sexism in today's world and that it's keeping young women down and making them want to "be more" to make up for their shortcomings inherent in being humans (who are, by nature, imperfect). Our society needs to learn to accept women for who they are, to not punish women for being born female, and to stop expecting them to compensate for their gender with résumés that, laid down flat, could reach Japan. Supergirls must completely scrap what society told them was "empowerment" and instead be true to themselves.

As such, in *The Feminine Mystique*, Betty Friedan urged women to find themselves in feminism . . . and that should also happen today. Feminism is not about wearing political buttons or going to protests (although you could if you wanted to); it's about living up to your potential and recognizing that there is a ton of power that is intrinsic to females. On one hand, being a feminist is totally easy, requiring girls to live their lives to the fullest, take advantage of everything being offered to them, and enjoy being female. On the other hand, it does challenge you to think differently about what you know: within feminism, you should try to recognize where you've found empowerment in strengthening guys' advantages. It's about buying your own drinks because you can, talking in your normal speaking voice when flirting (because, I've found, nothing says "submissive" more than talking like Smurfette), and understanding that you matter, for reasons other than being a sex object or being perfect.

Although you might be out ten bucks, an Appletini tastes much better when you've bought it yourself. Similarly, earning trophies and promotions and compliments on your beauty feel much more satisfying when you know that you don't *need* them to be important and loved.

chapter eleven

"So What Should We Do About It?"

Finding the Good in the Supergirl Phenomenon

....

Then Dorothy exclaimed, "Certainly you are as
good as you are beautiful! But you have not yet
told me how to get back to Kansas."
"Your silver shoes will carry you over the desert,"
replied Glinda. "If you had known their power you
could have gone back to your Aunt Em the very first day
you came to this country."
—The Wizard of Oz

It's not like the Supergirl dilemma is a total downer. For
younger women, the presence of Supergirls means that becoming a Supergirl is an option for those who aren't particularly
popular or socially comfortable, to be accepted by their community and embody the female ideal—another kind of female
ideal. On a more morbid note, as many adults live inauthentic
lives and don't really have that "Who am I?" crisis until their

40s, young women today have it out with their demons at a much earlier age, and if they do hit rock bottom during the throes of their Supergirl-ism, they have a much better chance of understanding who they are and seeking other kinds of fulfillment as adults. As Dorothy in *The Wizard of Oz* learned, she could have gotten back to Kansas immediately if she had known she had such power inside of her. And Supergirls matter—for reasons that have nothing to do with getting into college or having a good job or being pretty—but they need to explore themselves, and in some unfortunate cases, have it out with their demons.

For right now, dealing with the Supergirl dilemma is a tango: trying to be perfect is absolutely crippling for young women, but achieving is crucial to women's progress, whether it's electing women leaders and appointing female CEOs or simply living a happy, fulfilled existence. Working—in its various forms—is necessary for living a full life, but the balance between work and recognizing that work isn't life is what makes life worth living. Girls shouldn't have to be "super" to receive respect and attention; women should be acknowledged as human beings who are still lovable despite limitations and flaws. They don't have to go to Yale . . . the security and acceptance they crave have been in their hearts all along. However, for young women to find this acceptance, an overhaul of how we view them is necessary.

Allie, Age 20, George Washington University

Allie's a great girl: she's accomplished, she's interesting, and she's well on her way to some ambitious goals. If I were ever going to start an interest group in ten or so years and I needed a lobbyist who I knew would get the job done, I'd have her on the phone in a minute. Allie is at a campus where the young and privileged run free, but the "it" girls aren't so much the WASPy chicks from Greenwich with trust funds (like at many other schools in the elite private college league that GW seems to be in), which lends itself to a much looser social hegemony. As Allie said, the brown-haired suburban Jewish girls tend to be the queen bees. This is all well and good, except for the fact that Allie isn't really one of them.

During the time that I spend with her, I don't see her rabidly checking her phone for text messages the way my friends and peers do, and her phone doesn't ring; she doesn't wave to people she knows around campus, and her day-to-day schedule doesn't seem to include hanging out with friends. When we trudge through the puddles in Foggy Bottom, she doesn't really exude the shimmering, sunny vibe that, say, Pegah and Leah did. I don't doubt for a moment that she has friends and that she is in fact a *great* friend, because one of her friends came over to watch *The Office* and they spoke amicably about people who they mutually knew, and her best friend is her roommate who she lived with last year in a brownstone with five other girls. But I don't think she's the social butterfly of GW . . . which is perfectly fine!

What's endearing about the Supergirl phenomenon is that girls who aren't the most popular can still adhere to and embody a societal ideal. Allie probably doesn't go home for breaks with stories about partying with the children of politicians and political pundits in the dorms or being lovingly escorted behind the ropes of the hottest clubs in Washington's alcohol-drenched Adams Morgan neighborhood . . . but who cares! She's met household-name politicians and former presidents, networked with top GW university officials, and was graciously invited back for a second semester at her internship. Being a Supergirl allows her the flexibility not to have to be the most popular girl on campus, who swishes her hair as she walks and makes it a point to date a steady stream of fraternity presidents . . . but still be revered by family and friends. Even if she is a little bit cerebral, being a Supergirl exempts her from having to adhere to the somewhat superficial standards of what it meant to be an impressive female in yesteryears.

Whether trying to be perfect is more exhausting than trying to be popular is a subjective question . . . however, a fair one to ask. Is it more trying for Allie to make it to an 8am class before a day at her work-study job, her internship, club meetings, doing layout for the GW *Hatchet,* and cooking dinner for her hungry roommate than to be pressured to pledge a top sorority, attend to and impress a demanding and large group of high-profile friends at all times, have her hair dyed ice blonde once a month, and make sure that the gossip going around about her is factual and as positive as possible? Although there are obvious undertones of Supergirls being caged into overachieving, I think being pressured to do everything and excel in several subjects gives them a little more space for creativity than the previous roles for women, which required little originality.

I wonder whether Allie is threatening to her peers and this might prevent her from ascending the social ladder. While you must have quite an impressive résumé to even get into GW, some students take it a bit easier while enrolled in college and many students don't commit themselves to the schedule that Allie lives. And I could understand that if Allie's accomplishments did interfere with becoming popular, how Allie could be perceived as intimidating (despite being merely ninety-five pounds and speaking in the upper registers). She is almost ten years younger than her fellow intern and she's younger than most of her classmates because of AP credits from high school. Although Allie joked that I was more of an overachiever than she was, I personally found GW's little superstar to be a touch threatening: she has several internships under her belt; she wants to be a lobbyist, which will put her in a social and income class far exceeding the majority of Americans; and she speaks sternly and concisely, which given societal constructs of how young women are supposed to be cheery at all times, is sometimes a little unnerving.

GW's social scene is also fairly varied. Allie seems to fit in with an intellectual group (she's popular among the theater crowd and the school newspaper folk, and her best guy friend is a long-haired grad student), but around campus, there are preps and hippies and nerds, both old money and new money types, popular kids walking in gaggles (totally blocking the sidewalks . . . ugh!), and seemingly unpopular kids who walk alone. They all seem to coexist, and they probably all experience pressure to be the best at what they do. Although the Supergirl dilemma is consistently (and probably should be) construed as a negative thing, trying to be perfect does provide some sort of validation when straying from social norms.

The key to progress in the future is striving for a web of interactions and relationships where it's perfectly okay to be an individual and stray from the path of what you "should" do or the way you "should" live, without having to be perfect. Not to mention, in moderation the Supergirl behaviors that Allie has already mastered—functioning fully on little sleep, multitasking and juggling several activities and stimuli at once, speaking precisely and persuasively to those in authority positions, and always looking collected—are things that will totally give her a huge edge as a lobbyist. The key is just making sure that the weeknights and weekends are available to be unmanicured, awkward, and completely unscheduled.

Positive Supergirl Behavior and the Upside of Overachieving

We've been a little gloom and doom about the dark side of this overachieving phenomenon. But it's not all bad. With a measure of moderation, all the qualities that Supergirls have can absolutely propel them to success and happiness . . . and the presence of Supergirls actually does some good things for Generation Y and the millenials.

One of the coolest things about Generation Y—a generation so inundated with advertising, media, and stimulation overload—is that there is more than one role for teens. While virtually every teen aspires to be popular, unlike the 1950s depictions of high school and college, it isn't just about becoming the big man on campus (or the girlfriend of the big man on campus) . . . young people have been able to ease into different social groups where they can be more comfortable . . . and they get some credit for being "individuals." If a young woman attends a big enough high school or college, she can become the queen bee of the theater department or can be the popular kid within the honors society if she doesn't really have a chance of getting invited to the venerated soccer team parties or rushing Delta Delta Delta. Obviously, there is more validation awarded to teens who wear five layers of Abercrombie clothing, but at most schools it seems that kids can be cool within their own social circles. What's also cool about the Supergirl dilemma is that it's made it cool to be smart. While, again, being popular and graceful will always occupy that top rung on the social ladder, being the president of the National Honors Society at school or being known for your involvement with the College Democrats definitely carries some social capital . . . and that wouldn't have happened if overachieving wasn't the new black.

With that in mind, can a balance be struck? Can girls try to be collected and confident and perfect . . . but not slayed by it? If overachieving has a specific purpose—like running around like a madwoman organizing political events on campus to outdo the College Republicans or to keep a scholarship—is that overworking excusable?

Similar to Jenna, the first Supergirl we met who was nearly killed by her own drive, there was another girl I knew growing up who appeared to be perfect. She was a year older than me, and she was amazing. She had the second-highest average in her graduating class (according to rumors, she lost the valedictorian spot by a fraction of a point, which was a heartbreak for every girl in school rooting for her), she led countless clubs and was nominated for streams of awards, she played three sports, she was nice to everyone, and everyone (who wasn't jealous of her) liked her back. Growing up, when I was in an awkward situation or just wanted to *do something right,* I thought to myself, *What would she do?* She was impossibly thin, absolutely gorgeous, and constantly poised. She looked perfect all the time and never seemed to encounter any trouble.

And while some who resented her might have argued that her perfection was some kind of facade—that she was hiding something—I don't think that's true. I think this girl was so confident and happy that when she did face adversity or when she did get into trouble, she was sure she could handle it. And although she wore perfectly coordinated outfits from Abercrombie and Fitch and wore her hair down, shiny and blown dry almost every day . . . a few times a month, she would come to school with a bandana to cover her hair, in pajamas, and no makeup on, but carried herself with the same air of confidence that made you forget that she was in flannel. Although I can't remember that many instances, she'd say stuff every now and then that was awkward and stupid . . . but those listening didn't really register it because she was able to laugh it off. And I don't think that her "I'm-happy-calm-cool-and-collected" act—even when aiming for perfect scores in AP classes—was disingenuous. I think she was simply the most optimistic person I'd ever met in my life, who, despite the challenges she laid before herself, was sure of herself and happy. I think her parents raised her with a strong sense of self and to be powerful and kind . . . and she was rewarded for this by being able to be well rounded *and* healthy.

I met a few other overachievers who balanced work, school, social obligations, and having a life . . . who I don't think are Supergirls. I think they're immensely talented and accomplished . . . but I don't think that they're missing something inside that makes them search for more. And I think that's the balance! Girls can be busy and can thrive off of that feeling of "I have ten things to do in the next four hours before I need to crash into bed" if they're doing it *voluntarily*. Some people thrive off of being crazy busy, and if they're not overscheduling themselves to justify their existence and they're taking care of themselves . . . hey, go for it!

I spoke with Chelsea when she was a senior in high school; she had just received acceptances to Stanford, UC–Berkeley, and the University of Southern California, and had finally made the decision to go to USC. Just talking to her, I got exhausted. "I get up around 4 in the morning so I can shower, get ready for school, and be at school for swim practice by 5:30. Then I have school, and I have National Honor Society meetings and some other club meetings to go to, then I have swim practice again, and then I get home around 8 and shower again and have dinner and do my homework—I took *so* many AP classes this year. Then I try to get to bed around 11 or midnight, because I need to be up around 4 the next day!" Chelsea also volunteers at the local food bank and does triathlons in her "spare time." What was weird, however, was that Chelsea did not sound like an exhausted girl who was getting four or five hours of sleep a night and running from obligation to obligation all day. She sounded excited about what she was doing and privileged to have the opportunities to participate in clubs and such.

And here's the other thing: Chelsea sent me her college essay, which painfully discussed her father, an alcoholic, being in jail for much of her childhood, and how when he was released when she was 9, he had a heart attack literally as he walked out of the doors of the jail; he was in dying in the hospital a week later. Her family struggled financially, her mom was overworked, and she watched her older brother and sister grapple with grief . . . and their academic records subsequently suffered. Chelsea worked so hard in school because she was blazing her own path—not following in her father's footsteps and avoiding her siblings' fumbles—and trying to make a better life for herself. What indicates a problem in Supergirl behavior is that young women are stressing themselves out and taking on all these obligations for no reason—they don't have bills to pay or families to support or electricity that may be turned off—they are trying to fill some kind of inner void. However, striving toward a goal that wasn't available to someone's disenfranchised parents—even if it means being sleep deprived or missing some social interaction—doesn't seem too unreasonable to me . . . in fact, I think it's a really positive thing.

> "When I said I was taking a gap year during college, some people thought it was great, but no one understand why I was doing it . . . because that's not the kind of thing I'd do. . . . Life should be my classroom, not some white guy telling me what to read."
> **—Samantha, age 19**

Finally, when I look around New York, I see young women everywhere who are really living life. Sure, some of them aren't as mentally balanced as they could be (in terms of making time for themselves or appreciating their intrinsic value), but they're getting stuff done. Today's young women are leading in college and academia, are setting the dialogues in the publishing and nonprofit worlds, and appear poised to eclipse their male counterparts in previously patriarchal industries like finance and politics. Today's young women have learned the ropes of success . . . because of their overachieving in high school and college, they know how to organize, lead, and pull all-nighters without so much as rumpling their outfits. And those who have already dealt with the downside of the Supergirl dilemma—be it exhaustion, eating disorders, or realizing their broader inauthenticity—have the strength to overcome adversity and a new sense of who they are to help seize the day!

What This Means for Me

When I was in my midteens, I kind of always half expected that because I worked so hard and because I never really dealt with my problems, I would become an alcoholic at age 25 or 30. I actively knew that it wasn't really a good idea to work as hard as I did and to be as obsessive as I was about being productive . . . but it was a great defense. I knew that I was often kind of insecure and fake, trying to imitate behaviors of others who I admired and pretending to like people and fashions that I didn't. I also knew that I was in for trouble with college, having never found a school where I was comfortable and having taken my college rejections completely to heart (especially given that I spent the entire summer of 2004 studying for the

SAT). But I kept myself super-super busy and just absorbed myself in superficial activities, never really learning who I genuinely was. Because of my semester at SUNY–Stony Brook when I had to come face-to-face with my own inauthentic living at the age of 19, I have the rest of my life to live demon-free.

When school that semester ended, I spent the month of December at my mom's house upstate trying to find myself. I made sure that I slept ten hours a night. I painted for entire afternoons while listening to French music and Louis Armstrong. I stopped drinking coffee and gave myself lots of pedicures. I tried to stop daydreaming (I am an avid daydreamer). I took my dog on lots of walks and watched a lot of television. (In the eighth grade, I decided that it was appropriate to taper off my television watching if I wanted to go to Harvard [ha . . .], so by the eleventh grade, I had absolutely no interest in watching TV. And I never got to learn how passionate I was about the rhythm and precision of dialogue on TV, the formulas for plots and cliffhangers right before commercials! At this point, I have to curb my TV watching again, just because I would never get anything done again if I watched TV to my point of satiation.)

During the course of writing this book, I have really changed. Halfway through the writing process, I was confronted by my own inauthenticity that I'd been avoiding for years and I felt as though I was going to lose it. In the months to come, I had to relearn how to be human and figure out who I was . . . and it was one of the most important things I think I've ever done (and also one of the most difficult).

What I've learned in life so far—and in doing this book—is that everything is a balance. A young woman has to work with societal ideals if she wants to get jobs, network, and genuinely be accepted. We live in a commercialized, sexist society, so to a certain extent, some behaviors are required, like tweezing your eyebrows, having your teeth bleached when they get too yellow, and pretending to like certain people on the job. It's okay to wear makeup and shave your legs and be giggly . . . as long as you let yourself go Sephora-free for a weekend, stop getting Brazilian waxes if they make you bleed, and don't laugh at jokes that you don't think are funny.

But then it gets a little confusing. When you find yourself, you learn things that might surprise you. So much of my identity is wrapped up in being blonde, being Carrie Bradshaw-ish, and being overcaffeinated and micromanaged. After some serious reflecting, I figured out that if I was really being *me* and if I was really open to exploring my preferences, I would let my hair grow back brown, I wouldn't wear high heels or go tanning ever again, and I would stop drinking coffee and instead watch *a lot* of TV. Because I'm already pretty set in my role and I really like the attention I get for being blonde, feminine, and successful (I'm a work in progress, too), I'm not about to change. What I wish for the other girls out there—especially the younger ones—is that they'll have more opportunities to explore what being female means.

There's this running joke that there is some tribe in Africa whose members hit themselves really hard on the head with something heavy first thing in the morning so that their day can only go up from there. And I think something vaguely similar is going on for today's girls. The way our society, media, and marketers have constructed adolescence, there are bound to be problems for young people. And as we work to take on the problems that this media saturation and emphasis on superficial measures of worth have created, young people—particularly young women—are going to struggle a little bit with adolescence. But if we get those struggles out of the way early, we have our entire lives to live feeling complete and happy.

Personally, as my friends kind of anxiously await their quarter-life crises and the struggles that supposedly come with the 20s, the way I see it, post–eating disorder, post–adolescent angst, and post–college identity crisis, there is no more room in my life for struggles and there are no more things to worry about! I'm set for my 20s (and hopefully my 30s) to be a relatively nonturbulent, exciting time where I can go on all eight cylinders, learning and exploring and making changes . . . and making lots of time for the important things in life, like friends, family, boyfriends, and TV. I'm not going to become an alcoholic in my 20s because I warred, gloves off, with my issues at 19 . . . and I'm emotionally in a way better place now. Plus, having had to figure out the Supergirl work–partying balance in college, I learned that I get extremely bad hangovers that prohibit me from having a productive day if I have more than four or five drinks the previous night. Finding the healthy Supergirl balance is letting myself have those "productive" days to go to the park and play rather than work.

Prescription for Supergirl Success

Because of my constant overachieving and constant working (much of it done alone), I often felt like I had little to talk about with family and friends. I worked to look more interesting and accomplished, but often I had no clue who I was outside of my accomplishments. I'm quirky and loud, and I buy leave-in conditioner when I'm upset, but I have also spent so much of my life conforming to what I thought would make me perfect, so I didn't really know who I was. And that's not healthy! And I'm still working on it. . . .

I asked nearly every single Supergirl I interviewed what she does to "stay centered," stay relaxed, and stay healthy. I got a lot of answers revolving around sleeping in whenever possible on the weekends, doing yoga, calling Mom and sisters, hanging out with friends, having sex, drinking wine, exercising, shopping, reading trashy celebrity tabloids, and enjoying pets. One of my good friends, a "recovering" Supergirl in her late 20s, recommends making plans to relax, then relaxing as though it was another task to be checked off in a day planner, and then continuing to do that until relaxing feels more normal. Another one of my Supergirl friends makes a strict schedule for herself where she can only work for ten hours a day, and weekends are strictly for play. However, aren't these kind of like a Band-Aid to cover a bullet hole? What we need is to completely deconstruct the Supergirl facade and redetermine what it means to be validated. After all, Dorothy and friends from *The Wizard of Oz* traveled so far to get what they had inside of them all along, and Supergirls go to such lengths to find themselves in their accomplishments, when really, their personality and value are always inside of them.

Young women need to reevaluate who they are and why it is that they matter outside of what they've done and who they are. The things that they do should be for themselves, not to make others happy or to justify their existence. That's not what life is about!

On the following pages I've suggested some practical and some fairly simple (although not all are fairly simple) ways to decode the Supergirl dilemma.

"I feel like, we're young, this is our time to have fun!"
—Marie, age 19

For High Schools

• **Humiliation doesn't help.** Many high school newspapers publish a list of graduating seniors and the schools they are attending in the final issue of the paper; other schools give seniors pieces of construction paper to write what college they will attend in the fall and what their major will be to paste on their lockers. Not only does this create anxiety for students (*OMG, everyone who reads the school newspaper or walks down the hallway will know I'm a failure because I'm not going to Yale!*), it also creates an informal favoritism among students. It's important for the school and for the community to revel over the success of their students, but said practices only shame the students who are going to state schools or entering the workforce and discourage self-exploration and adhering to a person's own standards of success. Such pressure can have even more dire consequences: an April 2007 *Newsweek* article reporting on the immense tragedy at Virginia Tech University discussed how the gunman's ethnicity factored into his unhappiness and noted that some Korean immigrants heavily pressure their children to go to the Ivy League schools, and "'Local Korean TV' [in the United States] will even broadcast who gets into which college."

• **Reexamine the conditions for female students in high schools.** As much as we hold the traditional high school gender stereotypes to heart (the barely dressed cheerleaders, the football teams eating together at Hooters restaurants, winter "Hoball" dances), schools need to examine what kinds of messages they are sending young women about their prescribed roles in society. What is the point of working to get an A in AP calculus if the point of being female is to be a sex object? Or, how exhausting, to have to be both a brain and a sex kitten! Similar to high schools' approach to stopping drunk driving or not tolerating racism, schools should have assemblies on gender roles and what it means to be male or female, and teachers should take students' sexist remarks in class and in hallways to task. Teachers should also keep in mind that their female students have countless expectations to shoulder and should not dole out the pressure.

• **Encourage students to participate solely in activities they are interested in.** This will literally increase the hours in a day for students and make them feel more genuine (and Harvard knows a padded application when they see one). Recognize students who choose a specific extracurricular activity that they focus on and excel at, and encourage others to do the same; halfhearted participation in twenty clubs is a recipe for student burnout and enables perfectionist students to hog school leadership positions. Encouraging students to find something they are passionate about and to focus on it is the key to cultivating a more authentic and creative generation of young people.

• **Recognize students for alternative skills.** Although annual high school awards ceremonies are important, make sure that everyone receives an award or that certain students don't dominate the ceremonies. Because doesn't every student contribute something unique to the campus community? Excellence in drawing, poetry, or frankly, even making silly YouTube videos is just as telling as excellence in AP bio. And this is a stretch, but I can think of some delinquent kids in my high school who made others laugh all the time, cheering up the student body in the dead of upstate New York winters, and the sole recognition they got for their, um, talents was a lifetime of being chased down by the dean of students in charge of detentions, when really, someone should have said to them, "Stop being such a little delinquent and causing trouble . . . but you should try doing stand-up at the local clubs or getting an agent. You're really funny; you just need to channel this in a more positive way."

- **Discourage students from applying to more than eight colleges.** When strong students apply to twenty colleges (nineteen of which they couldn't humanly attend), it means more rejections for other highly qualified students who really aren't the ones best at handling rejection. Pick two reach schools, four good-fit schools, and two safety schools to apply to. Yes, it's fun to see how many Ivy League schools want a certain student, but it makes the entire college admissions process that much more difficult (and risky!) for everyone involved.

- **Encourage teachers to take an active interest in their students' lives.** I had teachers and a guidance counselor in high school who literally changed my life, who encouraged me to pursue journalism, who piqued my interest in language and foreign cultures, and who helped me realize feminism. However, there are an unfortunate number of young people who fall through the cracks, who don't have adults looking out for them . . . and an unfortunate number of teachers who dole out the pressure and seem to be trying to create an antagonistic relationship with their students. Adolescents really need to know that there are adults rooting for them . . . and teachers can be life-changing.

At Home

- **Remember that praise is important.** Parents must remind their children how important they are, how proud they are of them, and how proud they still will be of them if they go out for dinner and to the movies on a school night instead of studying. Give daughters validation for the things that matter, like having a great group of friends or being genuine. There are a few cocky kids who were slobbered with praise from their parents, but there are exponentially more who could benefit from a few "Attagirls!"

- **Pay attention to your daughter!** So many Supergirls are simply starving for recognition and want to be noticed by their parents. A biweekly or monthly date to Starbucks with your daughter takes just sixty minutes, but it will provide her with an entire adolescence of knowing that she has a support system.

- **Recognize the power of siblings.** While my sister and I always got along fairly well (especially considering that we're both loud, competitive young women spaced only two years apart), I never realized until I left home for college the strength that the bond between siblings can possess. My sister, Allie, who I now consider my best friend, is also the one person in the world whose life experience is the closest to mine, and her insight and feelings on the issues that I encounter mean the most to me . . . and I'm so glad I understand her value.

For Colleges

- **Give more financial aid.** Honestly, no one cares whether the microscopes are state of the art or that the petunias are well pruned. However, many students do care about the financial barriers to education. After all, is Mount Holyoke College or Smith really promoting that much progress or education if their degrees are truly only available to wealthy young women? Yet didn't Harvard and Yale reestablish themselves as pinnacles of higher learning when they made undergraduate education at their colleges free for students with a household income under $60,000?

- **Reexamine the pressures that college cultures put on female students.** Like high school, many college campuses are awash with sexist traditions. What kind of messages do 95-pound cheerleaders send to the female Ph.D. candidates studying biology? Do the fraternities and sororities—with their date auctions, misogynistic hazing rituals, and enforcement of rigid gender roles and antagonistic relationships between the sexes and the sororities—actually do anything for the campus except boost alcohol consumption? (I recognize that many Greek organizations are good and productive, but the ones I interacted with were so trite and stereotypical that I felt embarrassed for them.) At the same time, hire more female professors—they set an example for students to excel similarly.

For Girls

- **GO WILD!** Sort of. Keep your clothes on, but have tons of fun. After all, we're young. These are our best years. Enjoy them. Don't party too much, but party. On arbitrary nights when you and your friends are tired of studying (and your fake IDs didn't do you justice at the local bar), go to the 24/7 grocery store and fling one another down the aisles in shopping carts. Blare "Crash" by Dave Matthews Band and dance and spin around in circles in your living room. Allow yourself to be a little flaky— right now is the only time in life that you'll truly be able to get away with forgetting stuff and taking a week to return e-mails. Although it seems like a big deal now, odds are good that in forty years, aiming for perfect scores on state exams or a 2400 SAT will seem like a very, very dumb pursuit. Learn how to strike a balance.
- **Embrace feminism.** The word has an icky reputation, and it honestly occasionally merits its icky reputation . . . but most of the time, it's the key to living an empowered existence. Realize the power—actual power—inherent in being female. Challenge

that the doors to the kitchen in many sororities are locked at night to keep girls from eating and that the fraternities don't have house parents, but the sororities do. Consider if young women hopping on top of the bar and grinding with their friends when they're drunk actually makes them powerful, or if it just feels good because it garners positive reinforcement from guys. And question why it has taken us so long to get women leaders in government! It won't just be you challenging sexism: Rachel McAdams (star of *Mean Girls* and *The Notebook*) politely turned down the opportunity to be on the cover of *Vanity Fair* when she arrived at the photo shoot and found out that she would have to be nude with two other actresses draped like sandbags over the seated fashion designer Tom Ford, who would remain completely clothed. In 2007, Kelly Clarkson publicly protested when the all-male executives of her record label wouldn't listen to her ideas for her CD and concert tour, and she revealed to the media that people were only ignoring her ideas because the music industry is dominated by old white guys and she's a woman. Emma Watson (of *Harry Potter* fame) told *Parade* magazine in the summer of 2007 that she was a feminist and said, "There are too many stupid girls in the media. . . . I think sometimes really smart girls dumb themselves down a bit, and that's bad."

• **Talk with your friends.** Although consciousness-raising groups evoke an image of women with weird '70s-styled haircuts sitting on a shag-carpeted floor passing around a joint and talking about their vaginas, getting groups of your friends together to talk about what it means to be female can be incredibly eye-opening. Get a bottle of wine or make some fruity nonalcoholic drinks (my personal favorite? Equal parts cran-raspberry juice, diet ginger ale, and sparkling apple juice, in chilled martini glasses) and *talk* with your friends about the struggles you face and the things you think about. You can have topics of conversation ready, if you like, for example: "Were we explicitly told to be good?" "What does it mean to be powerful?" "What is a vision of our lives that we are satisfied with look like?" "Who should pay the bill at dinner?" "Do we cede power accepting free drinks at Ladies' Night?" "What does it mean to be female?" or "Can femininity be powerful?" Or you can simply plan to talk with your friends about being female and see where the conversation goes. You can even put the invitations to your consciousness-raising soiree on lacy doilies or do what you need to make it feel less weird, but having these discussions will feel so liberating.

• **Recognize the importance of relaxation and health.** Bodies, like cars and manicures and paintings, often require attention, repainting, and a little TLC. Give your body a rest, both physically and mentally. Sleep until you are satisfied, eat until you're full, and relax until you are rested. If your shoes are uncomfortable, stop wearing them. And make time for pampering: in my opinion, it has great health benefits. In fact, many local massage schools and beauty schools offer discounted services if you let students practice on you, so look into booking monthly hour-long massages, which usually range between $20 and $40) or half-hour $10 pedicures. I personally knew I wasn't doing a good job taking care of myself a few months ago when I was having constant backaches and didn't have time to read the seventh *Harry Potter* book when it was released. So, I started getting regular massages and *made* time to read It honestly was as important for me as my tetanus shot.

• **Consider therapy.** In working individually with clients in therapy, SuEllen Hampkins has learned that Supergirls can tone down their expectations for themselves and find happiness. "When we're able to identify this [drive to overachieve] as an issue for young women and we could pinpoint what expectations there were and how they were unrealistic and unfulfillable, we would come up with a client's own definitions of what a happy, successful life would mean to her. Often those things would be very different than what she was trying to live up to." Celebrities from Britney Spears to Mark McGuire have divulged how therapy has helped them, and according to a September 2007 *CosmoGIRL!* article, about a third of teen girls have been in therapy at one point or another, and 10 percent think therapy is "sort of cool."

For Everyone

- **Appreciate alternate paths.** Our society is fairly set on the idea of high school for four consecutive years, followed immediately by college for four consecutive years, followed immediately by graduate school for two or three consecutive years, and work for the rest of your life. We allow no margin for periods of relaxation, self-exploration, motorcycling through Europe, or taking a semester off to just figure stuff out. I know my adolescence would have been completely different if I had a year off between middle school and high school, and I really could have used a semester-long vacation before my junior year of college. A year or so after I graduate college, I am going to make an effort to live in Paris for several months and do nothing but prance around the cobblestone streets, wear poofy skirts, eat *tartes aux froimboises* in sidewalk cafes, and write poetry that probably won't be published. My career can wait a few months while I make memories that are going to be immensely fulfilling.
- **Make mistakes.** In my favorite song ever, Natasha Bedingfield sings, "We've been conditioned to not make mistakes, but I can't live that way!" Mistakes are an integral part of the human experience, and often the best things come from living a little dangerously and taking chances . . . and while sometimes those

turn into mistakes, they provide the opportunity for great richness and success. What if Bill Gates or Matt Damon hadn't temporarily disappointed their families by dropping out of college? We wouldn't have Microsoft or one of the best-looking actors of all time (mmm . . . Matt Damon)! For Jennifer, a 20-something Texas-bred *gal*, getting divorced was one of the most important things to happen to her. "I got divorced—I was married relatively early—and it was the first time that my life wasn't going along with this perfect image and this perfection strategy that I had in place, and it challenged my sense of doing things in the right order and doing things the way that others on the outside perceived it. It came at a pretty high cost. Making the decision to get a divorce, I really did think, *Wow, this is really a rupture in my "perfect" life.* But this painful situation actually became very positive." Instead of trying to constantly live up to a better version of her life, Jennifer found that being a divorced 20-something actually allowed her to experience strangeness and unpredictability: "I learned that I can't live my life on a schedule. I have to be open to the chances life hands me. And because I was no longer in this relationship, I could really embrace my creativity and experiment with who I was."

• **Live the most interesting life possible.** At the very least, you'll be able to talk about it at cocktail parties, but if you're lucky, your life will be a mosaic of chances, bizarre happenstances, and opening doors. Says Trudy Hall, the head of the Emma Willard School in Troy, New York: "I was accepted to Harvard and Stanford to do my Ph.Ed. (doctorate in education), and I knew that if I went to Harvard, it would be a familiar setting because it was on the east coast and more traditional, and if I went to Stanford, it would be on the west coast and would push my comfort zone a little bit. I opted to go to Harvard and had a wonderful education there, but I also knew that I missed out on some different experiences by not going to Stanford . . . experiences that I will never be able to have again." Says Cathy Wasserman, a New York–based life and executive coach: "Young women need to say to themselves, 'I am open to exploring the wonder of my life.'"

• **Eliminate the word perfect from your vocabulary.** . . . At least as it applies to people. No one is perfect, and every time in my life that I've tried to describe someone as perfect, she ends up having a breakdown or he ends up being a terrible dinner date. It's a dumb word and we shouldn't use it. Nix the *good/bad* dichotomy, too: those are appropriate words to describe a steak you order in a restaurant or the quality of cream, but not people.

• **Reevaluate what it means to be female.** We expect women to be nurturing and maternal. We expect women to be constantly happy. We expect women to be docile and not appear frazzled. We expect women to rear children, raise children, and still work and try to stop the pay gap. We expect young women to go to school, to lead others, and to fulfill all the expectations of them. We expect women to be perfect. We expect women to fulfill all stereotypes of them, yet break molds. The various expectations on women and stereotypes about what it means to be female are preventing them from becoming so much more than they are, even if they are already "everything." They could be really happy.

Going Back to Kansas

In researching and writing this book, I've realized that I've only begun to scratch the surface regarding the issues that young women face. I met girls from good families who, unable to receive thrill in their lives where they restrict food and force themselves to be "good," have taken to shoplifting for kicks. Young women list what they ate that day with disgust on walks with their friends down the city streets and blindly pass by homeless people who are actually starving—and not by pure willpower. I realized in my own life that my friends and I will lie about feeling okay and stable and confident in situations where we are none of those things . . . but we try to fake composure in front of the people who we're the closest to.

But being a woman is wonderful. As children, we can dream of being princesses, astronauts, movie stars, and doctors. Girls can innocently profess their love to their first crushes in the sandbox and get serious crushes on the cute science lab teachers in the fifth grade. Teen girls have the opportunity to experience the sheer joy available to them: first kisses, sleepless sleepovers, and trolling the mall for entire afternoons smelling the heavily cologned air in Abercrombie and Fitch and trying on piles of skirts but not buying anything. Young women can have baring relationships with their friends, whom they can profess their love to when they feel like it, cuddle with when they're lonely, and share the most intimate times and details of their lives. Women can grow human beings in their bodies, give birth to them, and have possibly the deepest relationship possible with that little person. Being female is a gift, and if I'd had the opportunity to choose my gender at birth, I'd voluntarily choose to be female.

Which is why all this murky stigma and tumult engulfing femininity is so awful. And what I think young women really need to do is start living for themselves. What's the point of going to Yale, graduating summa cum laude, and becoming a chief executive at a major cosmetics company if a woman real izes when she's in therapy at age 30 that she actually wanted to be an artist? Why should a girl dye her hair blonde if she thinks it actually looks better brown? Why wear high heels that give a gal huge blisters if she is a runner who relies on her feet to carry her (both literally and figuratively)?

We Supergirls need to start doing what we want, for ourselves, and ignoring the requirements put on us. And this is pretty radical . . . but then again, how radical is doing what you want? It's not rebellious, it's instinctual! Young women have simply been taught to silence their needs, when really, they should be their own first priority.

And when they start to listen to themselves, the Supergirls can grow up. They don't have to be Supergirls anymore. They can simply be women. And they can go to parties and drink because they like the feeling and dance because it's liberating and have sex because it's fun, but do it for themselves. They can finish writing that term paper (single-spaced at first, because when you make it double-spaced at the end, it's really a climactic feeling) and they can feel good about it because they did a good job . . . for themselves. They can get promotions and know that they earned them, feeling the title not as validation but as a compliment. They can love and be loved, not for the validation, but for the sake of breathing in the world's most magnificent emotion.

And then we'll have it all. . . . Or, is that even the goal anymore?

Suggested Reading Guide

There were a lot of different media—books, articles, even a poem!—that informed my writing of Supergirls Speak Out. If you're interested in learning more about overachieving, the politics of college admissions, adolescent psychology, and women's issues, check out these resources below!

Books

Bennetts, Leslie. *The Feminine Mistake*. New York: Hyperion, 2007.

Douthat, Ross. *Privilege: Harvard and the Education of the Ruling Class*. New York: Hyperion, 2006.

Dowd, Maureen. *Are Men Necessary? When the Sexes Collide*. New York: Penguin, 2005.

Friedan, Betty. *The Feminine Mystique*. New York: W.W. Norton, 2001. (original edition: Dell Publishing, 1963).

Golden, Daniel. *The Price of Admission: How America's Ruling Class Buys Its Way Into Elite Colleges—And Who Gets Left Outside the Gates*. New York: Random House, 2006.

Kindlon, Dan. *Alpha Girls: Understanding the New American Girl and How She is Changing the World*. Emmaus: Rodale, 2006.

Levy, Ariel. *Female Chauvinist Pigs: Women and the Rise of Raunch Culture*. New York: Simon & Schuster, 2005.

Martin, Courtney. *Perfect Girls, Starving Daughters: The Frightening New Normalcy of Hating Your Body*. New York: Simon & Schuster, 2007.

Pipher, Mary. *Reviving Ophelia: Saving the Selves of Adolescent Girls*. New York: Random House, 1995.

Quindlen, Anna. *Being Perfect*. New York: Random House, 2005.

Robbins, Alexandra. *The Overachievers: the Secret Lives of Driven Kids*. New York: Hyperion, 2006.

Roiphe, Katie. *The Morning After: Sex, Fear, and Feminism*. New York: Little, Brown, 1994.

Sessions Stepp, Laura. *Unhooked: How Young Women Pursue Sex, Delay Love, and Lose at Both*. New York: Penguin, 2007.

Tanenbaum, Leora. *Slut! Growing Up Female with a Bad Reputation*. New York: Seven Stories Press, 2003.

Zailckas, Koren. *Smashed: Story of a Drunken Girlhood*. New York: Penguin, 2006.

Articles

Reitman, Janet. "Sex and Scandal at Duke." *Rolling Stone*, June 1, 2007

Rimer, Sara. "For Girls, It's Be Perfect and Be Yourself, Too." *The New York Times*, April 1, 2007.

Poem

Robinson, Edwin Arlington. "Richard Corey." 1921.

A quick note about this poem: When I was fourteen and complaining to my mom that I felt awkward and that so many other girls seemed to be "effortlessly perfect," my mom suggested that I look up the poem "Richard Corey," by Edwin Arlington Robinson. A few weeks later, I did get around to Googling it, and the poem really got me thinking about the secret reality behind many of the people who "look perfect." "Richard Corey" is a perfectly crafted poem (a poem that I hope English teachers are teaching!) with amazing symbolism. But most importantly, its theme is a powerful one that I think today's young women can glean a lot from: there are often scary, heartbreaking secrets hiding behind the glowing exteriors of "perfect" people.

A Conversation with Liz Funk

You've written and published a book at the age of 19! Do you view your success differently now than you did when you were overworking yourself as a Supergirl?

Luckily, yes! I think at this point in my life, I can recognize that I've achieved stuff and can congratulate myself for it, rather than feeling as though I could always be doing more. I'm trying to allow myself to savor my success. There is definitely a vacation to Florida in my near future, but I don't think the old me would have considered completing a book sufficient reason to take a week off. Overachievers can be very funny like that.

Where do you draw the line between being an overachiever and having a healthy amount of ambition and drive? How can girls tell if they're working so hard for the right reasons?

I think overachievers work as hard as they do for the wrong reasons; when we see young women studying forty hours a week in high school and college, they're rarely trying to satiate a thirst for knowledge. They're often struggling to understand why they matter, and working too hard is a very convenient and accessible way to distract oneself from one's thoughts. Also I think a lot of what drives Supergirls is self-berating, which—hopefully—isn't something that drives all girls!

I think girls with a healthy amount of drive can still go above and beyond the call of duty in work or school or relationships . . . but they know when to call it a day and plop down on the couch with a movie when they're tired. For example, one of my best friends, Lauren, isn't a

Supergirl, even though she gets great grades, is a good daughter, a great friend, works two jobs, and is really skinny and beautiful. The difference between her and Supergirls, although there are many, is that if she has a night off from work and she doesn't have homework, she'll sit down in front of the TV and not feel guilty about it at all. It's awesome.

Was there a defining moment for you when you realized that you really needed to change your ways?

Yes, definitely. When I was a junior in college, I transferred colleges and left Manhattan to enroll at this huge public school on Long Island. I was put in a dorm that was almost all international students who didn't speak English, and the students in my classes had this major-award urban iciness to them. I had an impossible time trying to make friends, so I was completely socially isolated and completely alone with my thoughts. And what I realized was that I had no understanding of why I mattered or why I was special or important if I wasn't living in Manhattan and trying to be Carrie Bradshaw—ish and aggressively working on my career. I came face-to-face with myself and found that I had wildly low self-esteem and felt inherently boring. So I can definitely identify with the breakdowns that so many Supergirls described to me, because mine lasted an entire semester!

If someone had told you to relax at the height of your ambition, how would you have reacted? How do you think other girls can try to help a Supergirl who doesn't yet realize she is one?

I think I was at the height of my Supergirl self in the spring of 2007, when I was a sophomore in college. I had a really good friend who was always like, "Why do you work so hard? It's the *weekend!*" And I was always like, "I need to get my career rolling! I want to have this really fantastic New York life, and I need to *work* for it." Totally lame.

I think a Supergirl who won't admit her Supergirl habits needs to realize her problems at her own pace, and honestly, I'm really leaning toward believing that it is important for Supergirls to have breakdowns and realize the (extremely) hard way that they need to change. If a girl can nip her Supergirl self in the bud, that's fantastic, but I sense that the Supergirls who have breakdowns are better poised to do some very provocative evaluating of their lives. Even though it's emotionally painful, it's really amazing.

Do you believe that eventually young women can grow out of their overachieving tendencies as they mature, or do you think they have to come to the end of their rope before they realize what they're doing to themselves and can begin to climb back up?

I don't get the sense that when Supergirls mature, their Supergirl behaviors dissolve with taking on real responsibilities at work or with the routine of married life. In fact, I think Supergirls who grow older without confronting their Supergirl tendencies simply become the Supermoms we hear about in the media who make elaborate homemade Halloween costumes and cut their kids' PB&J sandwiches into shapes with cookie cutters for school lunches, even though they have a lot of other things they could be doing! The Supergirl pattern of spending so much time doing unnecessary things to distract oneself from one's problems can be evident in women of all ages, which is why it needs to be confronted when girls are younger!

How did *you* finally let go of your Supergirl ways?

A huge part of it was writing this book! So many of the young women I met really worried me . . . and inspired me! I also did an interview with life coach Cathy Wasserman for this book that honestly changed my life. She told me that young women need to "be open to exploring the mystery of their lives," and I think that might be the most important advice I've ever heard. There is so much out there to be experienced that is right before Supergirls' eyes, if they could back away from their MacBooks and hop off the treadmill!

I've been living in New York City for going on three years, but this is my first year living in Manhattan with a cognizance of my Supergirl behaviors, and I am having more fun than I've ever had in my life—I'm noticing just how exquisite the world around me is. To think that I'd been power walking past all of the amazing things in this city during my first few years of college!

Also, after I had a breakdown at SUNY–Stony Brook, I spent the following month-long holiday break at my parents' house in upstate New York sleeping ten hours a night, painting and listening to French music, hanging out with my best friends from high school, and devouring self-help books, to try to relax, cope and figure out who I was. I literally Googled "how to find yourself." It was weird for me to get in touch with just how insecure and depressed I was, but it was the most restorative month of my life. Fully finding myself ended up taking about six months of hard work of thinking and journaling and therapy, but it was so worth it.

Now that you've faced your issues, you seem confident that the rest of your life will be "demon-free." In trying to balance school, a writing career, and a social life, do you ever feel yourself reverting back to being a Supergirl—and if so, how do you deal with that?

It's hard to balance! A lot of days, my schedule is basically: get up and write, go to class, come back to my apartment, exercise and run errands, have dinner or go to a party with a friend, and then come home and write. But then I work really hard to make sure that at least two nights a week and one or two whole days a week, I do nothing all day except exactly what I want to do. But I'm happy now! And I think things are only going to get better from here. (Fingers crossed!)

But regrettably, I think I'm always going to struggle a little bit with this balancing act of being a recovering Supergirl. The best analogy I can think of I actually read in a women's magazine where Paula Abdul described her struggle with overcoming bulimia: with other addictions (alcohol, drugs, gambling, etc., etc.), you just stop doing it. But food and work are integral parts of life! People with eating disorders can't just cut food out of their lives and people with diseased relationships to work can't just stop working to nix the problem.

But it's not like I'm totally recovered. I'll know that I've completely distanced myself from being a Supergirl when I feel comfortable letting my hair grow out brown.

Do you think any of the girls you interviewed for this book are now on the road to recovery, having finally been able to talk about their issues?

Of the five "main characters" in the book, one just got married and moved to England, one got a job offer an entire semester before she graduated from college, one just received an award from her college for being so involved, one just started college at a good school, and I actually randomly just ran into the youngest of the Supergirls at my cousin's Sweet Sixteen party and she looked great. So, on paper, they still look amazing!

Whether they've come closer to coming face-to-face with themselves, I'm not sure. I think the younger girls I interviewed had a few real lightbulb moments as we were talking about overachieving and *why* they devoted so much of their time to attempting perfection, and I think that they may question their efforts today, but I don't know that any of them have fully confronted what they're doing yet. I think that they're all going to be wildly successful . . . I just hope that they can all be completely happy, too!

What advice would you give to girls who want to talk to their friends or family about the pressures they feel, but don't know how to broach the subject?

The power of honesty is overwhelming. Most parents are really perplexed by their daughters' behavior and would be eager to help . . . if they knew what exactly the problem was! I am a huge proponent of going out for regular Starbucks dates with Mom and just talking—it really keeps the channels of conversation open. Also, even though Supergirls have this disheartening tendency to compete with one another, I think friends are the biggest allies for young women grappling with the pressure to be perfect. Even though girls might feel uncomfortable confessing that their perfection isn't coming as easily as it looks, a girl's friends are supposed to be a really nonjudgmental audience.

What's up for you next?

I know I want to write for the rest of my life. I have literally almost ten more ideas for books that I want to write. I am also totally salivating about the idea of getting a job as a contributing editor at *New York* magazine or *The New Yorker*. And I also really want an apartment with floor-to-ceiling windows in a high-rise Manhattan apartment building.

But . . . I'm also keeping in mind that success and happiness comes in so many different shapes and sizes! I've been having a really amazing time living in Manhattan for the past year, and in meeting new people and trying out new activities, I've learned that there is a such a different rubric for success for people getting the most out of life. I've met a great number of people in the past year who are so creative and interesting . . . who either didn't go to college but are successful anyway, or went to awesome schools but make in the very low five figures because they're doing artsy stuff, or who plan to leave New York to travel for a year because the world doesn't actually revolve around New York! Because of their open-mindedness and the fact that they aren't berating themselves all the time, they are so successful! So, that's the vision of my life that I want to shoot for: being successful, but in a way that's very different from the way that Supergirls view success. Also, I want to live in Florida, Paris, and may Los Angeles for a little while, because, as said, I just stumbled upon this amazing realization that world doesn't revolve around New York City.

But actually, with all that in mind, I still want a contributing editor job and a nice apartment. Really badly. I'm always going to have a bit of Supergirl in me.

About the Author

Liz Funk is an award-winning freelance writer and political activist. Her writing has appeared in many magazines, newspapers, and online media, including *USA Today, Newsday,* the *Huffington Post,* and *Girls' Life* magazine. She regularly speaks out about topics pertaining to young women and Generation Y, and she's been quoted in *Cosmo-GIRL!,* the *Washington Post,* and the Associated Press, among other media outlets. She writes a blog about young women's issues for the Albany, New York, newspaper the *Times Union.* She is a senior fellow of Young People For, a branch of People for the American Way Foundation dedicated to mentoring young progressive leaders. Funk attends Pace University, studying English and women's studies in the Honors College. She was born in 1988 and lives in Manhattan, where for a long time she tried very hard to become Carrie Bradshaw and then learned it would be more fun (and more fulfilling) to just be herself.

Visit her at lizfunk.com.